PLAY...

The Foundation that Supports
the House of Higher Learning

Necessity may be the mother of invention,
but play is most certainly the father.

Roger von Oech

Ooey Gooey, Inc.
Rochester, New York
www.ooeygooey.com

ISBN # 0-9706634-1-2

Cover Design by Full Moon Advertising and Design
Inside Text Design by Andrew Curl

2003 Printing
Printed in the United States

2006 Printing
Printed in the United States

PLAY...

The Foundation that Supports the House of Higher Learning

By Lisa Murphy

For my brother Tom.

I had something to say – you helped me say it.

CONTENTS

Part One

Part Two

Acknowledgements

My appreciation to everyone who helped me give clarity, proper spelling and better grammar to the long-winded, run-on sentence that was the rough draft, including Judy Fujawa, Carolyn Kori-Sanders, Sarah Teres and Tami Obermann-Pouey. I could not have done it without your red pens, edits and careful eyes. I thank you for giving your time to my project. Again.

To my grandparents, Tom and Dorothy Whitworth, for providing the quiet refuge in the mountains where I could finally find the time, peace and inner quiet to begin.

To my folks, Jim and Laura Griffen for providing me with a playful childhood filled with many amazing memories that are with me to this day.

To Miss Mary, Miss Gerry, Miss Nancy and all the other teachers from Mary's Nursery School in Livermore, California – I thank you for the gift of a play-based nursery school experience. Those early years have come to serve as a guide and model for what I am dedicated to creating for the next generation.

And, last but not least, to the love of my life – Tom… I love you way high to the moon.

One down, one to go…

Part One

Chapter 1

Mornings With Mary

She opened the door and stepped out onto the porch. She was Miss Mary. My new teacher - my first teacher. She smiled as I scampered up the walkway to the front door. She bent down to my level and looked right at me. "Come on in," she said, "let me show you what we do here." She took my hand and we walked through the front door and into the world she created in that old house. So many things to do and see were waiting just for me.

The living room was filled with legos, wooden blocks, cars, carpet squares, dollhouses and hollow blocks too – a block builders paradise! Here children spent hours designing, balancing, measuring and engineering the architectural feats of childhood.

The former front bedroom, now art studio, was where creativity flourished. Here children were offered easels, palettes, brushes, paint, watercolors, crayons, paste (remember that smell?), home made playdough and clay.

The tiny bathroom was complete with child-sized toilets – no fear of falling in here! Right in the bathroom there were shelves of books to help pass the time, a small step to reach the sink and children's artwork gracing the walls!

Towards the top of the restaurant style, swinging door was a round window hole that made it easy to see the comings and goings of the kitchen – there was even a smaller hole cut out towards the bottom so the children could see in too!

The gathering area was in the former family room where Mary offered couches, pillows and beanbags. There was a flannel board, a piano and rows and rows of books! *Mike Mulligan and His Steam Shovel, The Little House, Caps for Sale, The Very Hungry Caterpillar and Babar the Elephant.* Books as far as I could see!

The former dining room now housed small square tables used for both activity tables and for snack time. Each was draped with a red and white checkered tablecloth and was surrounded by low benches and behind these tables, a door leading to the covered back porch... *there was more out there!*

The porch was a world all in itself. There were boxes of clothes for dressing up – long capes, high heel shoes, feather boas, raincoats, long "daddy" shirts, fireman boots, winter hats and party dresses. There were art easels out there too! A cotton string, the full length of the porch, was suspended above me. "The drying line," she said, "for your pictures." Long wooden brushes peeked out from recycled orange juice cans, which now served as paint containers. Extra paint and brushes rested on top of the wooden cable spool that doubled as a table! At the other end of the porch was a waist-high, wooden sand box filled with soft white sand. Next to it was a shelf where all the sand toys were kept. Scoops, funnels, egg beaters, flour sifters, wooden spoons, measuring cups and muffin tins lay waiting to be employed by a child's imagination.

We opened the screen door and stepped from the shade of the porch to the bright of the back yard morning. Ah, the yard – it was unlike any other. There were swings, ladders, structures to climb, bikes to ride, shovels for digging, hammers for pounding, ducks to chase and water to splash in. There were things to jump from, capes to wear, paper for painting, books for reading, dollies for washing, and there was a *boat!* A real one that we could paint on and pretend in! There was a sand pit for digging, bubbles for blowing and, right in the middle, a tall metal slide that was as high as the sun.

We stood there in the yard. Together. I didn't move. I just looked. Then, in a voice I can still hear, she gently let go my hand, bent down to me and said, "Go on now - go on and play."

I burst into the yard and spent the morning running around, dodging trees and leaping over ducks while playing tag and chase! I jumped over mud puddles, climbed the rope ladder that was suspended from the walnut tree! I read books on blankets in the shade, sang "Five Little Monkeys" and played "Ring Around the Rosie." I made new friends and giggled with them, splashed in the water, painted pictures at the easels and ventured through my new surroundings.

This was my first day of school.

I would spend the next two years with my Miss Mary, Miss Nancy and Miss Gerry. I would play hard, sing loud and make mud pies. I would climb trees, run with friends, jump rope and build with blocks. I would listen to songs, make puppets and draw pictures. Sometimes I would get mad and hit other kids, only to cry big tears when the same was done to me. I would make friends, push them away and then invite them to my party. I would be very loud and incredibly quiet. But today, this first day, while my shoes were still new and my lunch box still shiny, I would have snack.

No one could have guessed the impact this snack would have on my life. How could they? You see - I was a pretty average, normal child, maybe a little more talkative than some, definitely a little more active than most, but overall – a normal kid. Loved to read, sing, play, paint… do all the things that children enjoy doing. There was one thing though that really put me apart from other kids. One area where I was really different - my favorite snack. Not grahams, not PBJs, not applesauce or pretzels with oranges, but cheese. Hot spicy jalapeno pepper jack cheese. I could eat it on crackers, by itself, on bread, but my favorite way to enjoy the hot spicy cheese was when it was cut into slices and put on top of crunchy red apples. I loved jalapeno cheese with apples! No one really remembers how this "favorite" manifested, my mom though, seems to think that I went and visited someone and when I came home, it was my new favorite! Either way - snack arrived on my first day of school later on in the morning as our play came to a halt with an *invitation* to come and have snack. I say *invitation* because no one was *required* to come in for snack, no threats given if toys were not promptly put away, no general mandates to join the group at the table. Rather, an invitation was given to us as Miss Mary called through the dusty screen on the porch, "Come on in if you're hungry!"

I was hungry!

Her invitation prompted the hasty dropping of shovels and buckets back into the sand box, the jumping of children off the tops of climbing equipment, hoses being shut off, easel brushes tossed back into paint cups and bunnies returned to cages. It was time to eat. We had been playing all morning and we were *starving*. As we ran to the red and white checked tables and scrambled up onto the benches, parent assistants helped us pour water from small pitchers into cups while the children passed around the napkins. As I took my napkin the kitchen door swung open.

Miss Mary came out from the kitchen holding the big snack tray and on it were piles of crunchy red apples and slices of hot pepper jack cheese. I just about fell out of my chair! I thought all that cheese was just for me!

It was as though I had been invited to a dinner party, where, without knowing it, I was the honored guest and the hostess prepared all my favorite foods in order to show me just how excited she was to have me there! I looked up at Miss Mary as she put the snack tray down in front of me. She leaned in toward me and whispered in my ear, "We are so glad you are here."

Then she served me my snack.

I decided then and there I would become a teacher.

A Crystallizing Moment

Howard Gardner of Harvard University states that at any given moment of any given day, a grown-up in the environment could end up facilitating an experience that has a life-long impact on the child. He calls this a "crystallizing moment."

And the lesson here that we (as the grown-ups) need to remember is that we never know when these moments are going to occur. It could be Monday, Friday, the rainy day, the day we are in a good mood, the day we are in a bad one. Most of the time they happen when we aren't looking. Meaning – we are not running around all day "planning" and "creating" crystallizing moments. Many times they take place without us even knowing it, and they aren't always the big exciting moments either. There isn't a signal bell or loud trumpet! "Crystallizing moment occurred in room five!" No no no…. it's not like that. These are the moments when we are at our best, being honest, being present and giving the children what they need. Sometimes we don't remember the moments, but that doesn't matter - the children will.

I doubt Mary said to herself – "Boy I bet this cheese is going to be a big hit with the new kid!" No way! She was simply doing what she did best – she was aware of the children, their needs, their simple wishes and their comfort. I'm sure the casual (probably routine) call she placed to my mom sounded something like this: "Hi Laura! We are getting ready for Lisa's arrival! Since Monday is her first day at school and also first day away from you, we want her to have a smooth transition - maybe provide something that she really likes for snack - what's her favorite?"

A two-minute phone call that made a life long impact.

The *why* behind my work, the fire in my belly and the passion in my heart can all be traced back to when Miss Mary came through that swinging kitchen door carrying the snack tray...

It all started with the cheese.

Chapter 2

At Any Given Moment

Many teachers become teachers because of a teacher they had. At some point in their educational experience they were blessed with someone who took some extra time, went that extra mile, offered support and encouragement and did *something* that made a life long impact.

Remember this and take it to heart - *Never ever ever underestimate the impact of what you do!!* At any given moment of any given day *you* could make a lasting impression on someone. *You* could be facilitating a crystallizing moment! *You* could be their Mary! *You* could be their pepper jack cheese!

I became a teacher because of Miss Mary. The precious time I was able to spend in the magical place she had created is what inspired me to become what I am today. I, too, wanted a school in an old house with a huge yard where children could do all the things I was able to do. I wanted a place where I could give back what I got during my mornings with Miss Mary.

As I grew up I vowed to someday create a place for children where they could explore, create and simply *be*. Not be "getting ready" for something, not be "hurried up," not be forced or pressured to develop past their years. But to simply *be*.

I grew up, went to high school, college... sidetracked briefly by a short lived acting career and a two year stint at a performance college in Chicago - yet even there found myself taking child development and early childhood education classes! Watching children on the weekends, taking nanny jobs, volunteering at the local Boys and Girls Club and planning art activities for the children living in housing projects were all taking precedence over learning the lines for my upcoming show - it was then that I mustered up enough courage to ask myself why I was not *doing* what I was obviously so passionate about.

It seemed I was ignoring my calling.

I needed to do something different.

I decided to leave Chicago and return to California. Once settled back "home" I got involved with a program that would get me the training I needed to be a preschool teacher. I sat still long enough to earn my degree and kept the vision of Miss Mary in my head. While in school I saw things I liked and things I didn't. I daydreamed constantly about the school I would build - a place where grown-ups facilitated and guided in lieu of barking out orders and commands. I would create a place where twenty-minute schedules would be replaced with long periods of uninterrupted free time and where timers and whistles would be simply tossed in the garbage. At *my* school, rule-sheets would not be plastered all over the walls and children would be able to play outside *all day* if they wanted.

I would be an advocate for children because I would try with all my might to never forget what it was like to be little. I would educate moms and dads and give them permission to trust their instincts and each other instead of being pressured to succumb to the wills of prying neighbors, meddling relatives, and the ever present, powerful media when making choices for their children.

I would question what was served up as educational dogma and challenge "the way it had always been done." I would learn, grow, make mistakes, cry, scream and laugh. I would read everything I could get my hands on and find people to talk about it all with. I would ban product oriented cut out patterned art and would fire everyone who became a teacher because they like to tell little people what to do. But, above all, I would give back to the children what my Miss Mary gave me and would teach parents and other educators why play-based, hands-on learning *is* how children are getting ready for school!

I'm getting ahead of myself though.

This was going to take some time.

It was when my fantasy school came crashing out of the clouds immediately upon graduation that I realized just how long it was actually going to take.

My first real indication of the time it would take came when I began interviewing for my first teaching position. It became quite apparent that the early childhood educational environment I would be beginning my career in was quite different from the one I experienced when I was a child.   Upon graduating from college, armed with my degree and my naive passion to go out and be like Miss Mary, I learned a few things very quickly as I interviewed and toured local preschools and childcare centers.

First: the *idealism* of lab schools and college campus children's centers stood in stark contrast to the *reality* of day care.

Second: things such as bunnies and ducks in the yard, parents assisting at snack time, covered porches, slides and swings, half-day programs, outside easels and boats to paint were no longer the norm. Instead, early childhood environments were filled with long hours (for both teachers and children), no money for supplies, embalmed mail-order curriculum packets, patterned art bulletin boards, unspeakable wages, pressure to be ready for kindergarten and tired, over-scheduled children with frazzled parents.

Third: (the scariest of all my realizations) it seemed as though while I was in the business of growing up, going to school and completing my college education, all the Miss Mary's of the world had been mysteriously stolen away and replaced with the Laminated Ladies.

I encountered my first Laminated Lady when I showed up at my very first teaching job and was introduced to the woman who was going to be my "mentor." She would, according to my director, "teach me what I needed to know."

She had lesson plans that were laminated - from 1975.

She was my first exposure to this very recognizable breed of teaching professionals. You find them on preschool playgrounds standing away from the children, spinning their whistle-on-a-rope waiting for the blessed time at which they can blow it to call the children in from recess. You can find them inside the classrooms too. They are the ones wearing keys around their necks; keys that open cupboards containing the playdough, paper and markers. Many of them have twelve boxes lining the shelf on the back wall, each nicely labeled, "January" "February" "March"... and in each box are the activities to be done for each month, every month, with every class, every year.

Laminated Ladies have masking tape lines down the middle of the classroom to show children where to "line-up" and name-tags attached to the lunch table and circle carpet to show children where to sit. Laminated Ladies have a schedule for snack time, outside time, art time, lunch time and potty time. They are the bosses of nap time and the drill sergeants of circle time. In their world, preschool is boot camp for kindergarten.

I was astounded!

When I questioned what they were doing and why they taught like this they told me, "Times have changed Lisa! It's not all fun and games like it was when you were little. We have to *get the children ready* for kindergarten now! We must do *curriculum!*"

After three weeks at my new job, asking questions and getting nowhere, Laminated Lady sat me down and informed me that I better just "get with the program!"

Chapter 3

Getting With The Program

During my first few months of teaching I was faced with so many questions - What was I doing? Where were the mud pits, shovels, story times and upright pianos? Am I going to make it in this environment? Was the teaching style I remembered *really* no longer accepted? Had things *really* changed this much? Did I *really* need to get with the program? Why was I the only one in this place who seemed to think that things weren't right and that things should be different? I felt very alone. I was dangling off the side of a cliff, frantically trying to hold on to the teaching style I remembered. I *refused* to forget my memory of Miss Mary! I so desperately wanted to give back what I had received. I wanted so *badly* to be able to make the early years just as memorable for this new group of fresh-faced children as they had been for me. I wanted to give them their very own pepper jack cheese!!!!

But I was not yet strong enough. I was unable to hold on by myself and had yet to meet the people who would have helped pull me up. So I fell. And I fell hard. Down, down, down into the abyss among the Laminated Ladies. Upon hitting the bottom I saw that smiles had been traded in for whistles, laughter exchanged for line-up lines, and hugs replaced with idle threats to "call your mother!"

I spent three years with the Laminated Ladies; I acquired my own whistle, my own roll of masking tape (and the line that went with it), files of dittos and patterns and, among other things, a basket of songs that included such favorites as "Wash, Wash, Wash Your Hands," and "Safety Belts" which of course were all sung to the tunes of either "Row, Row, Row Your Boat" or "Jingle Bells."

I gathered a collection of catchy phrases to use with children such as, "I'm waiting!" "Sit still!" "SHHHH! Be quiet!" "1-2-3! Eyes on Me!" "Get out of the bathroom!" and, my personal favorite, "Criss Cross Apple Sauce!"

I made huge construction paper STOP signs to hang on activity centers to indicate to the children when a center was "closed." I strictly monitored lunch time seating arrangements through nametags that were contact-papered to the lunch table and spent my evenings cutting out patterns for art and photocopying dittos for "table time."

It took three years of being in the abyss with the Laminated Ladies before I realized that "getting with the program" was not my cup of tea. I started to question the educational practices that had been modeled to me. I began changing my mind about many aspects of teaching. I found new mentors. I read new books about education, children, learning styles and teaching philosophies. I surrounded myself with other educators who saw what I saw, questioned what I questioned and were willing to embark on this journey with me. I had taken my first leap into a larger world. I grew up a little and changed my mind a lot. I no longer cut out patterns or ran off dittos. I no longer said things like "Sit still and be quiet" because I knew that children did not need to sit on their bottoms with "eyes on me" in order to listen to a story. I ripped up my masking tape line-up line and threw it in the trash. I kept the whistle though – to remind myself of what I didn't want to be *ever again*.

I was able to crawl out of the depths of Laminated Lady World because I had learned skills, found tools and met people who could help me do it. Truth be told, the lessons I learned from falling into the abyss were more powerful than if I had stepped around it. I do not regret my experience with them at all, and, in all fairness, I did learn from the Laminated Ladies. It was not all bad, horrible and rotten, but it was certainly not how I wanted to be. They taught me what I didn't want to be and for that I am grateful. I was patient with myself and took baby steps at first. I didn't just jump up and fly outta there! It took time! I tried something new, felt confident, assimilated the change, and took another step. Pause. Reflect. What is working? What is not? Real change takes time. It is not fast. Don't think it should be. Fast paced superficial changes do not last because they do not allow for a full understanding of why the change is necessary. There must be a process of increased awareness and personal discovery.

After some time my slow moving journey began to pick up momentum. It was getting clearer. I knew where I was headed. It is said that you always go back to what you know first… it was time for me to go. I took my first step of my journey back to Miss Mary and the teaching style I knew first.

Chapter 4
Starting The Journey

As I began my journey of becoming the teacher I knew I was put here to be, I immediately realized that there is always something new to learn, a new skill to obtain, a new article to ponder and a more challenging book to read. But I didn't want to just gather up ideas! I wanted to *do it!* So I made a commitment to not just collect skills, ideas and lessons from books but to live the lessons and start putting them into practice.

The preschools and centers I worked in allowed me to grow and learn, but for the most part were not conducive to providing the children with what research shows they really need… Time to explore - not 20 minute time blocks. Clay and dough – not pencils and computers. Mud, sand and water - not table time dittos and worksheets. Lots of outside time, shovels, hammers and nails - not "television time" with monitors blaring the latest Disney video.

My administrators would say that they were supportive of me, and to their credit, I believe they were. However, the troubling thing about a preschool is that policies and final decisions are often determined and regulated by individuals who have no experience in child development. They are "business people," often very good ones at that, but many of them are not "child development people" and this can cause conflict. Teachers want to provide engaging experiences and activities for the children; the owners want to keep the carpet clean. Teachers want to say, "Rip up the damn carpet!" Many educators end up quitting in fits of unbridled frustration while directors are often caught in the middle, playing referee between the demands of teachers and the expectations of parents and owners.

I began to question the administrators, directors, site supervisors and owners. I realized that lip service paid to "the needs of the children" and "the power of play" and the ever-present mantra of "developmentally appropriate practice" was not the same as *doing it*! They talked about it, wrote about it in their brochures, advertised it in the newspapers and discussed it in-depth during prospective client tours, but no one, as far as I could see, was really *doing it*. But what became so incredibly frustrating and what seemed to make matters worse, was when the "vigilante teachers" like myself actually started doing it, our efforts were often met with letters of reprimand! We were asked to "come into the office" and statements of, "we don't do that here" came across loud and clear.

We continued to go back and forth as the debates ensued - teachers struggling with other teachers, directors with owners, teachers with owners, directors with teachers, parents with teachers. At some point during the madness I recalled a poster my college sociology teacher had in his office, "When elephants fight, it is the grass that suffers," and after some contemplating I realized it was time for me to move on. It was time to find a place where continued learning and questioning was permitted, where wonder and curiosity were more important than the carpet and where I would have the freedom to develop my teaching style and my philosophy.

As I began setting my sights elsewhere I quickly realized that there were not many centers out there where I "fit." Many centers were hiring, I could've gotten a job... but I wanted more. I wanted to find an environment where my philosophy and the school philosophy matched! That place that made me say, "YES!" as soon as I walked in. The centers that seemed promising were (of course) those magical places where the staff never left because they knew it was such an excellent place to be! Not yet did I have the funding to build a school so I did what seemed the next best thing - I opened a family childcare in my home.

Chapter 5

A New Beginning

My husband Tom and I moved into a house that had a huge yard with space for a garden, a sand box and a mud pit! The back yard was large enough for climbing equipment but it also provided many nooks and crannies for independent play and exploration. The children ate the wild raspberries that grew along the back fence and made adobe bricks by drying blocks of wet mud in the sun. We grew tomatoes and green beans, played in the dirt and splashed in the water. There were both independent and teacher directed art choices offered daily. We sang and danced, read books, painted pictures, built block towers, wrote stories and watched the bugs scramble in and out of the garden. We froze water to make ice and then noticed what happened when we put it in the sun. I succeeded in creating a place, small though it was, where children were celebrated and their interests honored. It was energetic, child-centered and play-based. I was pleased.

I began to document my observations of the children, their activity choices, the materials we used and the things we "did" all day. I challenged myself to be able to identify the *what* and the *why* in what I was observing in order to master the ability to articulate my belief system and my philosophy. No longer excused from debates and discussions because I was "new" or "green," I came into my own as a professional educator and found it of utmost importance to be able to both support and sometimes defend what I was doing in the classroom.

The documentation process I had adopted quickly led me to rethink my lesson planning methods. It now made more sense to plan activities directly related to the interests I was observing in the children, rather than simply providing random activities I pulled from resource books. Until this realization, I prepared lesson plans in accordance to the unwritten code of lesson planning. Here is the planning recipe I was given, and expected to follow, (and did) until I had my ah-ha moment:

Whether spoken or implied, this *is* what is expected. Unless of course you work in one of those places where the curriculum and lessons come in the mail

Lesson Planning

INGREDIENTS:

One weekend a month
Pen
Mounds of "activity books"

WHAT TO DO:

Give up one weekend a month. Plow through resource books for two days until you find enough activities for the upcoming month. Fill in the blanks of a lesson plan book. Pick out a few highlights to post on the calendar that will be prominently displayed on the classroom wall. Photocopy this calendar for the parents (ideally to be posted on refrigerators as reminders of field trips and other school-wide activities but rarely making it beyond the back seat or floor of the car). Try to overlook the latter. Submit the lesson plan book in to the director for review. Do the activities you said you would do. Repeat next month. And the next. And the next.

from a corporate office fifteen hundred miles from your center. In this case you simply do, month after month, what the man who sits behind the desk tells you to do. But I'm getting ahead of myself...

As I embarked down the journey of rethinking lesson planning and themes, I read a lot about emergent curriculum, theme webbing, child-initiated themes and the project approach. I watched how different classrooms handled themes and lesson planning, and spoke with teachers who said their schools had stopped using them. I inquired, questioned and outlined a new system. I did not simply wake up one morning and, in a fit of Sunday laziness, decided not to do lesson plans anymore!! I did the work and research first and then defined my new process: I allow my observations of what *the children* are interested in determine my next course of action. The children became the boss of the process. Not me.

What exactly does this mean? It means that instead of getting all of your activity ideas from a book, they are now obtained from the children. It means there is a lot of active observation going on. It means that teachers are watching what the children are doing and use that information to extend or deepen the process. It means teachers are taking notes, jotting down what they see and using that information to set up new interest centers, find new books and deepen the activity going on in the environment.

I began walking around with a little notebook in my pocket and a pen around my neck. What were they telling and showing me that they needed from this place and how could I get that for them?

A classroom that abandons the traditional agonizing monthly lesson planning ritual in exchange for the preparation of meaningful activities based on documented observations shows a commitment to both the development of the children and the quality of their program. A classroom that merely stops lesson planning because it's "dumb," time consuming or boring, shows a lack of commitment and dedication not only to the profession, but also to the children.

The *children* are the curriculum. Objective and detailed observation of the children's desires, activity choices, interests, passions and challenges will provide educators with all the curriculum they'll ever need. I no longer believe that curriculum comes out of activity and resource books - I believe these books are just that, resources. These books are tools to be used in conjunction with observations in order to deepen the exploration occurring in the classroom.

Authentic, meaningful curriculum does not come in a kit you buy at a conference, or a pre-packaged box that arrives in the mail. How could someone working in an office that is one thousand miles from your home or school have any inkling as to what your children need in their environment right now? How is a mail-order unit on snow applicable to a family childcare home in San Diego? How are mandated lesson plans from a corporate office in Kansas City really meaningful to a group of inner city preschoolers in Seattle? They aren't. They are easy. These prepackaged kits make life easier and present a façade of conscious planning when really all they do is serve as a substitute for active involvement with the children.

In the end, I opted for meaningful instead of easy. I stopped the monthly agonizing ritual of filling in the blanks of lesson plan books with random activities, circle time games and science projects. Instead I sat with my teaching journal after the children all went home and reflected on what we had done that day.

I made time every day for open ended, process oriented art projects – having easels both inside and outside to cultivate creativity. We sang songs together. I read stories to the children and they read to each other. Some of the children began writing their own stories. Instead of ignoring behavior problems, or superficially dealing with them through "time-outs," we talked through them, discussed our feelings and planted the seeds for effective communication skills. We rolled up our sleeves to squish and explore lots of sensory experiences. We provided time outside for lots of running around, gardening, watching birds fly overhead, catching rolly-pollie bugs, playing parachute games, climbing trees, jumping off big boulders and eating both pomegranates and berries right off the branches.

I thought about all of this at the end of each day and asked myself, "What did we do today?"

After some time I shortened the categories of my observation book to a list of seven words: "create, move, sing, discuss, observe, read and play." At the end of the day would ask myself, "Did we make time today to do all of these things?" If "yes," I would document what we had done. If "no," I would question (and document) why not.

The "seven things" (as they came to be called) became the springboard off of which we determined the experiences and activities we offered in our program. Everything we did was grounded in one of the seven things and everything overlapped. **The seven things was not and is not a checklist!!** It was not like the children came in each morning and we said, "Here's a brush, paint a picture!" (Create, check!), "OK now let's sing a song!" (Sing, check!), "Come over here and look at the bird nest Peter brought in!" (Observe, check!). Get my meaning?? **This is very important!!** Each of the seven things is not something to "do" for the sake of doing only to then hurry on to "do" the next one. It brings up images of tourists at Disneyland - Matterhorn, done! Space Mountain, done! Thunder Mountain, done! Parades at noon, 3:00 and 8:00, done! Meet me at the Castle rendezvous point at 9:30 sharp for fireworks! Roger! Over and out! Aruugh! They are so busy "doing" that they aren't enjoying the sights, sounds and feel of the day. The process is overlooked because there is too much emphasis on the product!

Use your observations to plan for the next day. This might mean sometimes going to a curriculum or resource book to gather an idea or two that would deepen or extend something that the children had shown (or told me) they needed or wanted, *not because I needed an activity to fill a time slot*. Sometimes it would mean displaying extra materials. For example, maybe I'd put magnifying glasses and plastic goggles beside the trays of seashells that had interested everyone since our trip to the beach. Or maybe I'd make different kinds of paper available during art time because finger painting was the favorite art experience right now. I might be wondering (aloud or silently) how the project might be different if we fingerpainted on foil instead of paper. How about wax paper? Shiny paper? Construction paper? If my notes indicated that two children who rarely used the sand box were suddenly interested in it, instead of trying to figure out *why* they were suddenly so interested, I would simply put extra buckets and shovels near the sandbox to facilitate their new interest and encourage their continued exploration.

I was the facilitator. My job was to provide them with the time and the materials they needed to deepen and further their explorations within the environment. We made time each day to create, move, sing, discuss, observe, read and play. This became the foundation on which we built our program.

Chapter 6

Teach Us To Read!

After our family childcare program had been up and running for a while, the group of children who had been with me from the start, (those who had followed me from the Laminated Lady preschool center to my home) began to turn four, four and a half, and five years old. One day, out of the blue, they began asking me to teach them how to read and how to write their names.

It really took me by surprise! I told them that they didn't need to know how to do that yet... "Go play!" I said. But they insisted I show them. I insisted they go and play! We went round and round. So, needing guidance myself, I turned to my bookshelf and re-read what Vivian Paley, Bev Bos, Maria Montessori and Sydney Clemens might have to say about this.

Would "teaching reading and writing" be an acceptable activity in a self-professed play-based, child-centered environment? Could...*would* I still be those things if we went down this path, or would it hurl me into the realm of those "academic-cognitive-getting-them-ready" programs that I so loathed? I had so many questions! I spoke with colleagues, read articles and even flipped through the pop-culture parenting magazines while deciding what to do. I found myself questioning why I viewed their request to read and write so differently than their prior requests for, say, cornstarch, more paper, fresh paint or a new story. Why was this so different?

I was, once again, at another crucial point along my professional journey. After many weeks of thinking, reading, talking and investigating, I adopted the "reading program" that Sydney Clemens references in her book, *The Sun's Not Broken, A Cloud's Just in The Way*. And while I imagine her essay on the trials and tribulations of working with inner city children in a neighborhood preschool was not intended to be a guide for teaching reading, the method she described spoke to me. It seemed right. So I adopted it.

Not being a "literacy expert" or ever having any experience in doing this before, I trusted my gut and went with my first instinct – they asked me to teach them to read, so I asked them what they *wanted* to read. It seemed to me that since they were expressing this desire, they might have something specific in mind that they wanted to read or write! Here is what we did: I invited all the children (one at a time) who had proclaimed a desire to read to tell me the words they wanted to read. Then I wrote these words down on 3x5 cards. The children kept their individual word cards in their very own word envelopes which were neatly stacked on the table *they* designated as, "the reading table." During the day some of the children would opt to spend time at the "reading table," just as they would spend time looking at picture books, building with blocks, walking to the park, painting pictures and squeezing playdough.

It became immediately obvious that the words they wanted to know were words that grew directly out of their daily experiences! Right in line with what educator Jane Healy states in her book, *Endangered Minds*, that "children need experiences to attach words to." I was witnessing evidence of this connection first hand.

The children who had been with me the longest were the ones who were excited about continuing to add words to their word envelopes. To these children I taught (with my apologies to the literacy specialists) what I called the "connector words": "at," "and," "the," "to," which allowed them to create sentences. The more words they added to their envelopes the more obvious the link between experiences and words became.

One child had a brother who was very involved with Motocross bike racing, his weekends were spent with his family watching his older brother race his dirt bikes. Interestingly, his word envelope contained words such as "jump," "hill," "helmet" and "crash." All of the children wanted to read "daddy," "mommy," "house" and "dog." This wasn't very surprising as they all had one! The only child who wanted to read "baby" was the child with the new baby sister. I was amazed.

So we read. The process continued. The connection between words and experiences became very apparent. Younger children would declare their intention to read too – so we'd start a word envelope for them, but usually their interest didn't last. They weren't ready – *the direct experiences would need to come first*. Later on they would attach the words. Those with word envelopes were never ever forced to participate in this "reading process," and we didn't make a big deal out of those who did. We did not advertise our program as one that would "teach your child to read!" We did not list "reading skills" or "writing strategies" on our informational brochure. A child who had started a word envelope was not coerced or directed to "spend some time with his cards." It was just another part of what we did at the program, no different than the mud pit, the dress up area, the sand box, the stacking pegs or the block zone. It was a springboard off our foundation of making time each day to create, move, sing, discuss, observe, read and play.

After years of providing experiences the children were ready to start attaching words to them.

The first group moved on to Kindergarten and within a few months the calls began. I was not expecting these calls. My colleagues were not getting these calls. These were calls from Kindergarten teachers asking me what I had been *doing* with the children all day. Teachers announced to me that some of the children who had been in my program were walking around their new classrooms saying things like, "Been there done that! Been there done that!" One teacher specifically demanded to know what I had been "doing with them" seeing as I was just a (gasp!) family childcare provider.

A typical call went something like this:

"What were they doing all day with you?"

"Playing," I said.

"No, really."

"Really! We spent most of the day playing."

"What do you mean, *playing*?"

"We read stories and books, we sang lots of songs, painted pictures, played in the mud, ran around, played tag, planted a garden, did lots of science, squished shaving cream, played in the water each day, went on some field trips, you know – the usual preschool stuff."

"But some of them are *reading*."

"Some of them were ready."

"Yes but what did you *do*?"

"We played."

Clearly we were getting nowhere. I, who was *just* a family childcare provider, was clearly holding out on them, the professional elementary educator!

What was my secret? What did I do? Was there a special diet? No dairy? Lots of fish? Oh please, do tell the source of the expensive curriculum package you must have surely ordered from an educational guru! "Tell us!!" they demanded!

I hung up.

Of course they were doing well in school! Why did these people seem so surprised? These children had been given time to be children and time to do the things children do. They played! And by having spent years doing so, they went on to elementary school ready for more because their foundation was so strong!

And it was then that I had my major A-HA moment, my epiphany, my "Eureka!"

The foundation of play supports later learning!

I know we all *know* this, but I was now a first-hand witness to it, not just regurgitating facts pulled from research and articles to appease the resident naysayers. Every building needs a foundation or it will fall down! This *playing* is the foundation that is supporting the house of academics – the house of higher learning! Playing is the glue, or, rather, the cement that keeps the foundation of early experiences intact. The foundation itself is made up of all the things we had been making time for the children to do: creating, moving, singing, discussing, observing and reading. Playing became the cement that held it all together.

I had made some long strides on my journey but this was a huge leap for me. All of a sudden what I was really put here to do became very clear. I needed to develop this idea further. So while continuing to make time each day to do the seven things I began an in-depth exploration of *why*. I knew this exploration would encourage me to continue to grow both personally and professionally. It would increase my knowledge, strengthen my program and allow me to support my views while speaking with teachers, parents, providers and school administrators. I was walking the walk and learning how to talk the talk. I was gathering fuel for my fire, I was reading everything I could get my hands on, attending workshops and seminars and discussing views with colleagues. In the fall of 1996 I decided to make the time and financial commitment to attend a four-day national early childhood convention in Dallas, Texas.

I never would have guessed that my trip to Dallas would end up changing my life.

Chapter 7

Strengthening the Foundation

In the fall of 1996 I attended the National Association for the Education of Young Children's annual conference that was being held in Dallas, Texas. On the morning of the first day, a workshop called something like, "Ooozey Runny Drip: Messy Ideas for your Sensory Table," was being presented. The description in the conference program said to come and experience messy gooey things for your sensory table tub, handouts and recipes will be provided! OH MY GOSH! HANDOUTS with recipes!! I was running through the convention center because I knew that everyone attending the conference that morning was going to attempt to squeeze into this workshop! You know that any workshop at a conference that has to do with art, hands-on activities, sensory recipes, messy play, and especially any workshop that has a description stating, "handouts and recipes will be provided" is enough to cause a small stampede. This conference was no exception.

An hour before start time the workshop room was already filled to the brim with anxious attendees. There was a line out the door of people trying to get in! It looked like opening night of a highly anticipated movie release! I was in the back of the line but KNEW I needed to get in the room! I slowly (but surely) squeezed and "scuse me'd" my way into the room.

I worked my way down the aisle of chairs and through the sea of people. As I approached the front row - BINGO! I found an empty chair right in the front! I sat down and introduced myself to the people around me. The room was buzzing with excitement – you could feel the energy! Everyone was anxiously awaiting the handout that was sure to be filled with tons of new ideas.

So we waited. And we waited. And waited...

Suddenly someone shouted, "Hey! Where's the presenter?"

Just then, a NAEYC representative approached the podium. "Umm," she said, tapping the microphone, "Hi, I'm one of the conference volunteers and I'm sorry to say that we don't know where the presenter is. We knew that this was going to be a popular workshop, and, well, since there are so many of you here, let's give her a few more minutes."

She left the riser. People started whispering, they were getting restless. Where was she? Where was her stuff? Where were the activity demos? Where was the hands-on stuff? Where were our HANDOUTS?? I half jokingly tapped the arm of the woman sitting to my left, "Geez," I said, "I could talk about this kind of stuff. I do it every day with the kids at school!" She looked at me, "Well, why don't you get up there then." I looked back. I was silent. I paused, and then said, "Alright, I think I will!!"

So I did. I got up on the riser, took the microphone and said, "HELLO, my name is Lisa Murphy, and I am NOT the presenter (I didn't have the handouts). I was expecting a workshop filled with new ideas for messy, squishy stuff for my sensory tub – is that what most of you were expecting?"

700 heads nod up and down followed by a resounding "YES!"

"Well," I continued, "I am a family childcare provider in California," at this point a woman sitting in the front, who I later found out was from Colorado, stood up and cheered, "Yeah! Yahoo for family childcare!"

"And.." I smiled as I continued; "I do a lot of hands-on stuff everyday with my kids. So, since the presenter isn't here, I thought I could share with you some my favorite hands-on, messy activity ideas. Sound good?"

Again with the nodding.

There was a minute of chaos and then we started. And, to be honest, the next hour is really a blur – I don't really remember what I said, or what I told them. But, based on the dozens of letters I received from family childcare providers, preschool teachers and directors all over the USA for four months after the conference, I think it's safe to say that it was informative and fun! I know I shared some of my favorite messy things to do. I'm sure I told a few stories, shared some things that worked and some things that didn't. I solicited ideas from the crowd and everyone who wanted to say something did.

Workshop participants were asking questions, laughing and frantically writing down all the ideas that were being shared. The energy was great. The time flew by and as we wrapped things up I thanked them all. Thanked them for sticking with me, for sharing their stories, suggestions and activity ideas and, most of all, thanked them for allowing me such an amazing opportunity. Then with no prompting or signal or anything, they all stood up. They clapped, they cheered, they offered me jobs, and even asked if they could come see my school! They stayed after and asked me questions, and a few people yelled out, "DO YOU HAVE A BOOK???" I was awe-struck, amazed and about six feet off the ground.

Throughout the rest of the conference as I walked through the halls of the convention center to get to my workshop choices, I heard, "There she is, there she is!!! That's the girl who just got up and *did* it when the presenter didn't show up!"

I was beaming. The lesson here though, and what I took with me from Dallas, was the true understanding of what is meant by "the more you give, the more you receive." It would have been very easy to have jumped up on the stage, "done" the workshop, enjoyed the ego stroke and then gone home. I knew I had to do more though. I felt (and still do feel) as though an opportunity was placed in front of me and I decided to grab it and RUN!

So the *end* of the conference was the *beginning* of my new adventure. I flew home from Dallas knowing that it was time to do something. It was time to start giving back – it was time to start doing some workshops. After coming home and doing some research, I started my company and called it "Learning Through Adventure." While still teaching and doing family childcare I also began presenting hands-on art and science workshops at weekend conferences here and there and slowly came to be referred to as "the ooey gooey lady."

A while later Tom and I found it necessary to close our in-house family childcare program and relocate to a smaller home. We moved into a little beach cottage in San Diego where I continued working with children by subbing and mentoring in local preschools but spent most of my time focused on developing my workshops. The occasional weekend presentation at local child development conferences had morphed into an exciting fulltime professional business. I was invited by many wonderful schools, agencies and individuals to conduct in-service trainings, community seminars and conference keynotes all over the country. These speaking engagements allowed me to bring my message of child-centered teaching and the importance of the foundation of play to thousands of teachers, parents, family childcare providers, and school administrators. While doing so I became connected with my personal commitment to assist educators in rekindling the fire in their own belly and the passion in their own heart. I wanted to help them remember why they get up every morning and do what they do.

While the beach cottage was nice, it was very small and the business was growing fast. We had fax machines on the kitchen table, file cabinets in the dining room, client information taped to the mirror in the living room and product assembly tables lined up in the bedroom. I wanted to do family childcare again and the business obviously needed room to grow, so we purchased a home and opened another childcare program. We ran the Ooey Gooey® Workshop business from the den and opened our "large licensed facility" in the playroom that was attached to the kitchen. Our license permitted us to enroll twelve children, so we marketed the program and began hiring staff.

We enrolled babies, toddlers and preschoolers and the program was up and running. We facilitated the program during the day and did seminars and workshops in the evenings and each weekend. As time passed the childcare program became a working representation of what I was out on the road talking about. Our focus changed from simply providing childcare to that of seeing our philosophy in action. Our initial ideas surrounding the importance of play and of the "seven things," which previously seemed to be not much more than brainstorms which had been frantically scribbled in notebooks and on walls and napkins to someday "do something with," had turned into a fully developed childcare program and philosophy. The making of time each day to create, move, sing, discuss, observe, read and play no longer served simply as a guideline for lesson planning. Within our "seven things" we found not only the ingredients of a strong early childhood program, but of future school success and a love of lifelong learning. Years of observations, along with a thorough investigation of the research, uncovered the vital importance that early experiences have on the lives of children.

It was time to start spreading the word.

Chapter 8

When Does The Playing Stop?!

Open any research data base on the topic of "play" and you will find the evidence our *heads* so desperately need in order to support what our *hearts* have known for years - play is the foundation for future school success. By attending child-centered, play based preschool programs with an emphasis on social and emotional development (as opposed to those of the "skill and drill" variety) children *are* getting ready for school.

Children who spend their early years in academic oriented preschool programs focused on the accumulation of skills - dittos, worksheets, computers, memorizing phone numbers and flashcards and other activities designed with the sole purpose of "getting them ready" are in fact, not doing so. In her article "How Do Your Children Grow?" author Susan Black tells us that researchers have identified that around fourth grade you can easily walk into a classroom and identify who was in what kind of early school environment simply by the behaviors of the children in the classroom. The children who had been in rigid academic models are stressed, high-strung, aggressive, depressed and don't want to be there anymore. On the flip side, children who had been in play-based, child-centered preschool programs do better than their peers academically, are able to communicate with teachers and friends and are often creative problem solvers.

Some of us worry though that our children will get "stuck" in the playing part and will never move on, never amount to anything and, god forbid, might still be "just playing" when they are forty!!

I am reminded of a woman I encountered at a workshop once who stood up from her seat in the back row and frantically shouted to me, "But – *when*, just when does this playing *stop*!!??"

I calmly told her, "Hopefully never."

People sometimes tell me that by allowing children to play we are not providing them with a quality education. I have heard that in *their* day children went to school to learn reading, writing and arithmetic. No attention was given to playing in the classroom, "we did what needed to be done!" True. I do not doubt this. It is, however, very important to point out that in their day, they also had, roughly, a good six or seven years of playing *prior to entering the classroom*! Playing in the neighborhood was how "children got ready for school."

Economic and social conditions have changed though and many of today's children are spending their early years in nursery schools, preschools and childcare centers and do not have the "playing in the neighborhood" experience that their folks did. The six or seven years of honest to goodness free play experiences, polliwogs and tadpoles, bike riding, stick ball, kick the can, jump rope, sand boxes, picnics, family outings, fishing, mud pies, lemonade stands, climbing trees, vacant lots and tree forts in the back yard that their parents had in their yards and neighborhoods needs to be replicated in the early childhood environments where their children are growing up.

Of course our parents and grandparents were reciting, memorizing and doing sums in first and second grade! They had *six years* of play that created a strong foundation upon which were built the walls and windows of reading, writing and arithmetic! Playing comes first, academics come after.

Children today are NOT being given the same opportunity to develop at their own natural pace. They are expected to start "learning" and "performing" as soon as they emerge from the comfort and protection of the womb; "How much did he weigh?" "Is she rolling over yet?" "Does he sleep through the night yet?" "Can she tie her shoes?" "What preschool was he accepted into?" The competition begins immediately and it is *fierce*. Children are stripped of their right to play because of inappropriate pressure to begin accumulating a bunch of tricks they can then show off as though they were a part of a dog and pony show! "Count to 50 for Mrs. Barnes," "Tell Mr. Davis your colors," "Show grandpa what a good speller you are!" "Play your new song on the piano for Auntie Beth!" "Dance for grandma!" "Show daddy your flashcards," "Sit!" "Jump through the hoop!" "Roll over and play dead!," "Speak – woof woof!".

Congratulations, your education has begun. Here is your biscuit. Good dog.

When there is pressure to build a house without regard to the foundation that supports it, *it will fall down*. The same is true with our house of higher learning! We need to expand our own knowledge by realizing that play is not just an idle waste of time. We must stop thinking of time set aside for playing as time being taken away from something else – something deemed (by grown-ups) as "more important" such as academic preparation and school readiness. Play in fact supports school readiness! Play is NOT separate from learning! Our foundation of creating, moving, singing, discussing, observing and reading is held together by play. Play, if you will, is the cement holding our foundation together and it is this foundation that will, in turn, support the house of higher learning.

We all want what is best for our children. But what we are often *sold* as best has nothing to do with what our children really need. Kits and packages designed to make your child better, faster and smarter are nothing more than products that people get paid to sell. Contrary to what their marketing and advertising departments claim in their glossy magazine spread and during their high-pressure radio spots, they do not care about your *children*. They prey on your *emotions*, your *concerns* and your *desire* to do what is best for your children in order to *sell you their product*. All they really care about is your credit card number. We *all* want to see our children in big, grand, academic houses. But when we begin building walls, windows and second stories on a weak or absent foundation, what is going to happen?

Having all the good intentions in the world cannot make up for the fact that there is little or no support holding up our structure.

The foundation of play supports the house of higher learning.

Chapter 9
Meaningful Experiences

Adding and subtracting comes *after* the counting of rolly pollie bugs in the grass. After the listening of sound patterns made by pots, pans and rhythm sticks. After figuring out if there are enough oranges for everyone at the snack table. Not through memorizing sums from flashcards.

Writing comes *after* the squishing of playdough. After squirting spray bottles to make prints on the fence. After using three million sheets of paper for scribbling shapes and spirals. After the banging of marker tips, over and over again, on hundreds of sheets of paper. Not by purchasing lined paper and chubby pencils.

Reading comes *after* hearing many stories while sitting on a comfortable lap. After learning how to hold a book right side up. After having experiences that were often mirrored in favorite books. Not by purchasing flashcards.

We must locate a balance between the extremes of "Activity Annies," who on one side, don't do much more than prepare and provide children with the superficial, random, "cute" experiences they gathered up at the conference last weekend, and the "Laminated Ladies," with their whistles, timers, letter of the day dittos and colors of the week worksheets. Sometimes our pendulums swing too far in the opposite direction when we begin changing our minds about how we want to be with children. Be patient. Take your time. It can take *years* for your pendulum to find center ground where the blending of concepts and experiences comes naturally to you. Challenge yourself to continue growing and learning while finding your center point.

Spending time each day creating, moving, singing, discussing, observing, reading and playing strengthens the foundation that will support the house of higher learning. It facilitates social and emotional skill development as well as the *linking* of concepts to experiences in order to assist children as they begin making sense of their world. It is this *linking* towards which we are ultimately working. When the children jump off rocks, we mention "gravity."

When they see flubber oozing out of a suspended berry basket and slowly drip towards the floor, we mention it again, when balls go up and then come down we say it again. I do not expect the preschoolers to "get it," but I do know that if meaningful experiences are provided on a regular basis, the memory of the experience will trigger understanding when the concept is brought up again as they move on to elementary school. Out of these experiences come words, language and an understanding of the concepts. But the experience is the starting spot. And the experiences need to be *real*.

What is my vested interest in learning how to sort rocks by color or size, line them up, count them, or spell R-O-C-K if I have never held a small one, never climbed on a huge one, never gathered any at the beach, never felt with my fingers how some are so very rough and some are smooth like glass, never went on a hike and collected a few or never threw one into a puddle and counted the ripples? Children learn in the here and now! In their book *Developmental Continuity Across Preschool and Primary Grades,* authors Nita Barbour and Carol Seefeldt inform us that children do not have the capability to think abstractly until they are almost twelve years old! Therefore, every time we expect them to be interested in things (concepts, themes, activities or ideas) they cannot see, touch, taste, hear or smell right here and right now, we are expecting something that is developmentally inappropriate.

I remind my teachers to ask, "Can I bring *it* to them, or them to *it*?" If the answer is no, *it* more than likely does not belong in a preschool classroom. In the winter, if it doesn't snow where you live, why would you spend time talking with preschoolers about it? You might say, "But Lisa, it is a theme we do each December! What should we do?" I suggest either finding someone to truck some snow down from a mountain for you or taking a trip to the snowy mountain with the children and their families. If however, neither of these are realistic options it might behoove you to consider an activity or experience which is *more appropriate to your environment!*

A sensory tub filled with grated ivory soap is not snow! It's soap! White playdough is not snow! It's playdough! To children who have never been in the snow these materials cannot (and will not) take on these abstract associations unless forced by the adults! I must share a story – a woman who attended one of my seminars in Phoenix approached me on the break saying, "I gotta tell you something! It's about the idea of it needing to be real. I was raised back east but my children were raised here in Phoenix and every December their teachers would make playdough snowmen and big white coffee filter snowflakes to hang on the walls and decorate the classroom. I finally said – forget it! Next December we are going to Philly so they can see the real thing! So we get to Philly in December and one morning it's snowing hard! I woke the kids up and we go on the porch to watch and as my five year old daughter comes outside she looks up at the sky and," she continued, "her face simply fell. She looked disgusted! I didn't know why! I told her, Look honey look! Look at the snowflakes! And my daughter instead looked at me and said, Mama - the ones in Phoenix are so much bigger."

I rest my case.

The daughter – who for five years was exposed to 6 inch, 12 inch and even jumbo sized 24 inch COFFEE FILTER snowflakes - thought for sure she was being cheated when she saw the real "little ones" in Philly.

The *real* must come first! All subsequent abstract understanding is based on the initial experience of the real. And while the experiences are important it is also vital that we remember that there is so much "learning" that can be attached to the experiences we provide children. Remember, playing is not separate from learning! Instead we work on blending the concepts with the experiences.

Take apples for example. Imagine this September your program is planning on spending some time exploring apples. What kind of learning is taking place when children are encouraged to cut the apple (*dividing, math, estimating, small motor development, life skills*), make applesauce (*more math, counting, kitchen chemistry, measuring, changing from a hard solid apple into mushy sauce*), count the seeds (*math skills and small motor development to grasp them and pick them up*), plant the seeds (*gardening, patience, importance of water and sun, caring for a living thing*), cutting apples in half to make apple prints on paper with paint (*creativity, science, color mixing, art*), cutting then in half the other way to see the star (*observation, differences, similarities*), to chart and graph on paper who likes green ones yellow ones or red ones (*math, estimating, counting*).

Think of the *language* you would hear in a classroom filled with preschoolers whose teacher brought in basket after basket of real apples for them to experiences. Imagine, if you will, that the teacher wrote on the board all the words she heard the children calling out and saying to themselves and to each other as they ate their apples: *Red! Bruised! Crunchy! Sour! Sweet! Sticker! Green! Stem! Worm! Hole! Seeds! Star! Juicy! Dry! Mushy! Smooth! Bumpy! Sticky! Tart! Hard! Nasty! Smell! Big Bite! Taste! Smooth! Small! Big! Color! Shiny! Yellow! Round! Leaf!*

WOW!

Now imagine if the experiences during the same apple exploration time frame were limited to coloring books, dittos, identical construction paper apples hanging on the bulleting board, a few related books on the bookshelf, a basket of plastic toy apples in the dress up center and some flashcards in a box by the circle time carpet. To someone peeking in this room through a window it may *look* as though the children are *learning* about apples, but come on! *How much learning about apples can be going on if there isn't even one real apple in the room!*

What senses are being developed with a fake, plastic apple? What understanding deepened with a photocopied ditto of an apple to color? What language heard in the room where the children's experience of "apple" is limited to a flashcard? Would you hear Juicy? Sweet? Red? Seeds? Would you hear the expression of lively descriptive language in a room where real, red, juicy, sticky apples with long stems and green leaves had been replaced by a 3x5 card that had the word "apple" written on it?

No way. Impossible. Children need experiences to attach words to.

We can no longer overlook the importance of early experiences. Having the opportunity to engage in real, meaningful, hands-on experiences, as opposed to cute, fluffy time fillers, dittos, computers and worksheets, is how children begin to unlock the secrets of their world. The experiences children need are the ones that will allow them to construct a strong foundation that will support their house of higher learning.

As parents, educators, play group leaders, teachers, grandparents, family childcare providers and administrators we must make time each day for children to create, move, sing, discuss, observe, read and play.

I wrote this book to share with you the reasons why.

Part Two

Chapter 1

Make time each day to...Create

I have a theory that art has become a receipt for childcare. No longer is art done for art sake, but instead, all of the pieces of scribbled paper going home, the hundreds of easel paintings, the craft projects for holidays, the kiss good bye in the morning with the sugary request, "Make a picture for mommy today!" serve instead as proof to parents that the children *did something* at school today.

After talking with teachers and observing similar interactions in many schools in many cities, I have come to the conclusion that art has become the method by which parents are provided something tangible (a receipt) for the money they spent on tuition.

There are many reasons that this concerns me. First – what about the children who do not use art as their creative outlet? *It is important to realize that creating is not limited to the visual arts.* Many children enjoy painting, using watercolors, markers, glue and other art materials. Some do not. These children would often rather build with blocks, put puzzles together or play dress-up in lieu of doing the day's project. Yet they are often coerced into "making something today."

When children are "made" to do art, the intrinsic value is lost. Some children are simply not interested in art projects! Instead, they build enormous block castles, make detailed and intricate lego creations, mold animated playdough sculptures and prepare mud pies in the sand box. They design maps and go hunting for treasures in the yard. They link together all 100 pieces of the train with a story and tale for each turn of the track. They direct the drama of the dress-up corner by monitoring the "lines" and "roles" played by each baby kitty and mama bear. These children are also creating. "Proof" of it, however, doesn't make it home via cubbies or art files.

My very first baby step in dealing with this predicament was to purchase a Polaroid camera. The pictures I took of the children engaged in both art and non-art activities were posted on the walls, tucked into envelopes and sent home, taped to doors and contact papered onto the windows. It seemed to decrease the frequency of questions such as: "Where is their work?" "What did they make today?" and "Why doesn't my child paint?"

With the availability of digital cameras you can take photos, print them out or even e-mail them to the parents while they are at work. This sends a powerful message to the children and parents alike that all creativity is valued and appreciated, not just the art projects that are stapled to the bulletin board.

Photographs of various kinds of creative projects serves as visual documentation of the many things children enjoy doing while at preschool. Partnered with parent education, photographs serve as a helpful tool when talking about the "learning" that springboards off the open-ended, creative experiences you are providing.

My second concern is for the children who *do* enjoy art but whose creative impulses are often stifled by grown-ups that appear to be more worried about the carpet than the creative process. As I mentioned earlier, it is here that teachers, directors and parents often go to battle. When so many people are working together it is almost impossible to make everyone happy. Directors are caught between meeting the needs of owners, administrators, teachers and parents. Teachers sometimes must choose between doing exciting art projects and getting in trouble for children having red paint in the hair. Parents want their children to have fun experiences at school, but don't want glue on the children's jeans. Teachers provide open-ended creative experiences but are questioned and challenged as to how the children are being "prepared" for kindergarten. Teachers might provide engaging sensorial experiences, like ooblick and flubber-gak, but are warned to watch out for the carpet. Splatter art and finger-painting will often get teachers in trouble because clothes get dirty.

After a while, some of us just flat out stop providing these engaging experiences. It becomes easier and less stressful to do brainless cookie-cutter art and cut-and-glue projects than it is to fight the fight. So we cut, the children paste. We photocopy, the children color. We throw up our arms in defeat when the projects that now begin going home are the dittos and "receipt style" projects we avoided doing in the first place and we sigh and shake our heads in frustration because we don't understand why some parents seem to actually prefer them.

OK – stop.

Take a deep breath… slow and easy, in and out. I could feel your pulse start to race and your blood begin to boil. Go make a cup of tea or get a cup of coffee and sit back in a cozy chair. Calmer now? Good.

You need to ask yourself two very important questions and spend a minute or two really thinking about them before answering them honestly:

Question #1: Who is the art for?

Is the art being done for the parents? School visitors? Directors? Administrators? Owners? Or is it really by the children for the children?

Question #2: Why is art being done?

To fit into the weekly theme? To fill up the bulletin board? To go home in the art file? Or because the creative process is understood and honored?

Once, while co-teaching in a three-year old room, I watched children paint on glass jars for a holiday project. Most of the children used many colors and covered their entire jar. However, one child, Nick, made one big blue SPLAT on the side of his jar and announced that he was done! During naptime, I cringed as I watched his teacher "finish" his jar.

While studying to become early childhood educators we were all taught the importance of "Process Not Product." Yet how many of us actually stopped to think about what that really meant as we randomly selected art projects out of resource books to fill up our lesson plan book? Did we really understand the importance of process as we stapled twenty-four, identical, cut out, teacher prepared, child colored, paper plate owls to the bulletin board? Probably not.

The process of creating anything takes time. When cooking you need time to read the recipe, shop for the ingredients, prepare the ingredients and put everything together. Time is also necessary to actually cook or bake the meal. When time is limited we do something quick and easy like microwave meals or fast take-out food. Although this faster process might relieve us of our hunger, it is not often as enjoyable as a meal made when time is plentiful, savored and shared with friends over a long drawn-out evening. The same is true with creative art experiences. When there is enough *time* and the *process* is appreciated, children can make one, two, three even fifteen sponge paintings! The grown-ups are focused on the creative experience and providing adequate materials instead of only being focused on the final product and schedule taped to the wall.

So in one camp we have adequate time, appropriate materials and teachers that value the process of being creative. By this we mean that the brush strokes of red watercolor paint onto the paper are valued just as much as whatever the child might eventually announce he was "making." The art you see on the walls is as varied as the children in the room. You might see various kinds of easel art, many collage projects, many scribbled sheets taped or stapled to the walls. You will not see identical projects lining the bulletin boards. You will see a celebration of individual creativity, not conformity to a set pattern or example. This room values process oriented creativity.

Meanwhile, in the camp down the hall, we have tight rigid schedules, limited materials, and a focus on the final product (what is being made) as the most important part of the creative process. In our "product oriented camp" we see art that "looks like something," with everyone making an identical construction paper spider, turtle or cow. All the creations will be hung up on the bulletin board. Together. In a line. If using clay or playdough all will make a pinch-pot. If something new is introduced you will hear, "Watch me, this is how we do it." You will not see a lot of individual expression because the end product is what is valued - not how we got there. Therefore, in order to get the "correct" product you will see lots of teacher created examples, teacher led activities and children copying what teacher demonstrated as the "right way to do it."

It can be very challenging and time consuming to establish a child-centered, process oriented program. However this is our goal, so let's look at some things we need to work on remembering as we begin the process:

Tip #1: Each Project Will Be Unique

This means that as you work on emphasizing process instead of product you will no longer have bulletin boards covered with eighteen identical penguins and you saying, "But I let them glue the eyes wherever they wanted." Why? Because, again, the focus is on the process of creating, not having a set and determined finished product in mind. Want to do a gluing project? No problem – this time though, instead of cutting out all the pieces and requiring or expecting the end result to "look like something," simply provide time, materials and guidance and see what the children do with the glue, collage scraps and construction paper you set out for them. Each child will create something different and unique. That is the beauty *and the purpose* of the creative process.

Tip #2: Art Cannot Be Forced

You cannot "make" children do art. Creativity flourishes when activities are done for enjoyment not when they are forced or coerced. One time that I "forced it" really stands out in my memory – it was Mother's Day. The children were finishing up their Mother's Day projects and the director of this particular school actually came in each room to make sure that each child had "made" something for mama that would be presented at the Mother's Day Sunday Brunch. In my room all of the children had made hot crayon melting cards, all of them that is, except Patrick. Patrick just wasn't an art guy and I was intent on not "making" him do something. My director came in and wanted to know why Patrick had not completed his project. I explained to her that he was really into Legos and that I had thought of an alternate idea for his present – I would take a picture of him building one of his Lego towers and we could tape the photograph into a card for her. She looked at me over her thin, wire rimmed glasses and insisted he make the same project as the other children. I resisted, she insisted – we went back and forth for a few days until I finally just said, "Forget it! You win!" I went over to Patrick and sat with him for a minute, watching as he intently built with his Legos before breaking two of my own rules: #1: I interrupted a child who was actively engaged and, #2: I was about to coerce a child into doing an art project.

"Patrick," I said, "we're making cards for our moms today. Come on over and make a crayon melting card for your mom." He looked at me, put his Legos down, stood up and shuffled his feet over to the warming tray. He picked up a paper, grabbed a red crayon and pounded three dots, bam! bam! bam! onto the paper. He lifted the paper off the warming tray and thrust it at me saying, "Here Ms. Lisa! I'm done!" before running back over to his Legos.

So much for a heart felt emotionally charged project.

Later that month the crayon melting project was out again. This time Patrick was not in the block area building with Legos. He was pacing in front of the art table, stalking us, back and forth. He watched for *days* as the children melted crayons on different kinds of paper; but he never participated. Finally, one afternoon he called out, "Hey! Ms. Lisa! Are we making these for our moms?" I was silent for a minute, recalling the reason for his question and the Mother's Day events of a few weeks past. "Patrick," I said, "you can make them for anybody you want."

He grabbed the next available chair and made about twenty of them! He used foil, he used wax paper, he used scratch paper and construction paper! He dropped a few little crayons into the warming tray and watched them slowly melt away in the heat. He made fast scribbles, big circles and tiny ovals and on the very last paper he wrote his name with a melting red crayon. Then, picking up all of his creations, he walked to his cubby and stuffed them in announcing, "these are all for me!"

Tip #3: The Smaller the Child, the Bigger the Paper

Emphasizing the process means having H-U-G-E sheets of paper available. No more dittos, patterns and cut-out art. Instead, big sheets of paper for lots of open-ended art! Try butcher paper, art paper, newspaper, scratch paper, old desk calendars, copy paper, or even donated paper. For a while I didn't pay a dime for paper – I asked local businesses for donations. Here are some ways for you to possibly get free paper:

- Call the local newspaper and ask if you can pick up the *end rolls*. End rolls are too small to use in the printing equipment but contain enough paper to last a classroom for a long time.

- Ask a local architectural firm if they will donate their recycled *blueprints* – the back of the blueprints is a large sheet of white paper, and the designed side is neat to look at too.

- Paint on *newspaper*. Adults like white paper, children don't care. Really.

- Ask your local office supply store if they will donate the dated *desk calendars* at the end of the year.

- Contact a local print shop to see if they generate an amount of *scrap paper* that is large enough for your use. Sometimes you can score huge sheets of *cardstock* when they are done with projects, sometimes you can even get the cardstock end rolls! Keep your eyes peeled!

- Another idea is to keep your eyes and ears open for your clients who work in companies that are changing *letterhead* designs, phone numbers, addresses, etc. The paper is 8½ x 11, not really designed for art projects per se (too small), but excellent to have available for all the dramatic play writing that occurs each day! The year our county divided up from one area code to three was expensive for the business owners who had to keep changing letterhead - but the local preschools made out like bandits!

After receiving any donated goods, be sure to send a thank you note. Fill it with drawings from the children along with pint-sized handprints and enclose some photos of the children using whatever the donated item(s) were. Not only is this good manners, it almost guarantees a repeat donation when you make another request.

Tip #4: Not Just Paint Brushes Anymore!

Continuing to focus on the process of creating means seeing the possibility of painting with things other than paintbrushes. For example, try painting with any of the following: Golf Balls, Marbles, Kitchen Brushes, Baby Bottle Brushes, Strawberry Baskets, Squirt Bottles, Toothbrushes, Plastic Toy Cars, Fingers, Noses, Legos, Plungers, Bath Puffs, A Fish from the Butcher, Magnets, Tennis Balls, Dog Toys, Spackle Spreaders, Window Squeegies, Fly Swatters, Brooms, Trikes and Bikes, Snails and Sponges.[1]

Provide big sheets of paper and have some of the above-mentioned materials available. Add a few paper plates filled with bright, washable paint and watch the creativity fly!

Tip #5: Be Aware of "Creativity Killers"

While reading *The Creative Spirit* by Daniel Goleman, Paul Kaufman and Michael Ray, I came across a list of "creativity killers" which had been compiled by Teresa Amabile.[2] My appreciation goes out to her for generating such a clear outline of what we want to avoid while encouraging creativity. I have taken the liberty of including for you here, a few of the "creativity killers" we might find ourselves struggling with as we work with children. Please note that I have taken her list and elaborated on each of the "creativity killers" by adding my own anecdotal commentary. Please note that "Creativity Killer #8 - Baby Gap Syndrome" is of my own creation.

Creativity Killer #1: Surveillance and Hovering

When children are constantly under observation, their creative urges often go underground to hide. Think about this, if you are painting, perhaps drawing, maybe writing a new poem, would you want someone standing over you watching every move, every sweep of the brush and every stroke of the pen? Would you want them asking a lot of questions and commenting? Probably not. *Hovering gets in the way of the creative process.*

Provide children with materials for creative expression, give them time to explore and use the materials, then back off.

In our programs we have a place where the children can engage in what I call "free flow art." In this area items such as colored glue, scissors, markers, crayons, recycled paper, masking tape and hole punchers are available all the time. We call it the "creation station" and it is the place where children can literally create whatever, whenever. See if you can carve out a space for a creation station in your environment. In addition to many other art activities offered through the day, this center is "open daily" for creative exploration and imaginative play.

Creativity Killer #2: Evaluation

When facilitating creative expression we want to develop intrinsic motivation, not pressure to produce solely what others want, or what pleases teachers. Resist the urge to say, "What is it?" Resist the urge to really say anything about their creations.

If a child comes running to you saying "LOOK! LOOK! LOOK!" Then do just that - look look look!! The child did not say, *"Look look look and please make a comment."* If a child says, "Do you like my painting?" Put the question back to them and say "Do you like your painting?" I will often then turn the paper around or upside down and ask, "How about when I hold it this way? Or this way?" "Lay down and tell me if you like it better when I hold it over you." Practice this… say it with me – "How do YOU like your painting?" It's hard! But it's also a habit that can be broken.

While on your journey it is vital that you ask yourself this question: "Whose needs are being met by my comments?"

Why do we feel the need to gush over each scribble? Each painting?

Once while working as a mentor teacher in a preschool classroom, a little girl was creating truly lovely easel paintings. However, when she completed a picture, instead of announcing what a beautiful picture she was painting, or lavishing her with praise or gushing over the colors she used, I simply asked her if she needed any more materials. She'd respond "yes" or "no" to my offerings of more paint or paper, and kept on working. Later in the day (she was still painting), her teacher came over to her and remarked about how lovely and beautiful her paintings were and how she should be so proud and boy her mom will be so pleased! Do you know what she did?? She took the black paint and poured it all over the picture she was painting, turned away from the easel and didn't paint anymore while I was there.

Cultivating intrinsic motivation becomes key as we encourage children to contemplate their own creations instead of paying so much attention to what others say or think about them.

As hard as it is, you must try with all your might to refrain from making evaluations, and to practice NOT commenting. Remember that our actions really do speak louder than our words. YES! We want to be supportive! YES! We want to be encouraging! And the best way to show this is by asking, "Can I get you some more paper?"

What better way to show support and encouragement then by offering more of what they need to continue doing what they are doing.

Creativity Killer #3: Over-Control

An excess of micromanagement can be frustrating for the adult and the child. Take the issue of children's names on their artwork. I have seen teachers get completely *out of control* because the child doesn't want their name on their paper. When children acknowledge they are "done," I encourage my teachers to ask the child, "Do you want your name on the paper?" If they say "yes," the teacher then asks, "Where do you want your name?" Then they write it wherever the child indicates. If the child says, "I can write my own name," we give her the pen. If a child says, "I don't want my name on my paper," we leave it alone! We might inquire if they need help hanging it up to dry, or ask if they'd like some more paper, but that's it! There are no control battles over names on work and *no one sneaks back to write it when the child isn't looking.* Children know their work and will keep it if they want it.

We also discourage making models, samples and examples for the children. This includes not drawing for children.   When we draw for children all they end up doing is copying what we, the grown-up, drew. If you currently draw for your children I want you to know that this practice, too, is nothing more than a habit.   When the time is right, you will work on breaking it.   You can take a "baby-step" and start by changing the hand you draw with. If you are left handed, use your right, and vice-versa. When sitting with the children do not draw for them anymore, simply copy what they have drawn using your non-dominant hand.   Eventually you want to work towards encouraging them to create independently without needing you right there to do it with them.

Independent creativity begins to emerge when you enhance the art area with colored paper, pens, markers, rulers, tape, glitter, colored pencils and glue. Creativity flourishes when you continue to encourage their creations by asking, "do you need anything else?" Be patient and gentle with yourself and by all means give yourself time but make sure you are working towards the goal of not drawing for them.

Copying what the teacher did is not art nor is it being creative, it is the regurgitation of someone else's idea. Instead of saying, "This (holding up example) is what we are all making today," try just putting the materials out for them to experience and explore! A morning spent squishing, molding and poking clay does not have to turn into everyone bringing home an identical design! When adults over-manage children's art it can lead to the children into thinking that originality is a mistake, (we are *all* making candy canes) and exploration (no, no, do it *this* way) is a waste of time.

Rhoda Kellogg, child art expert, reminds us that adults who encourage copywork and forbid or discourage spontaneous scribbling may harm the child's development in learning as well as in art. Her observations suggest that the child who has frequent opportunities to draw without a lot of adult interference learns faster and increases his cognitive ability more than he would if he was denied the opportunity.[3]

I once saw a little poem hanging in the art area of a preschool classroom that I was visiting. Unfortunately I didn't have any paper to copy it down so I tried to remember it as best I could; it went something like this:

When you

Draw it for me

Cut it for me

Paste it for me

Put it together for me

All I learn is that you

Do it better than me

I think this says it all.

Creativity Killer #4: Restricting Choice

If the children are painting with roller brushes and someone yells, "I want the flyswatter!" unless there really is a true, good, honest reason that you can't go get the flyswatter, go get the flyswatter! Telling the child "no," or, "I can't right now," or, "we aren't using flyswatters today," or, "I'll get it tomorrow," when there is really no reason you can't just go get it right now, squashes a creative urge and an opportunity for expression and exploration.

Frequent comment to this is, "But Lisa, if I get Tammy the flyswatter, everyone will want a flyswatter!" Or the infamous, "If I get something special for David then they are going to all want something special!"

What is so wrong with that? What else on the day's agenda could be possibly more important than providing what they need in the here and now to deepen and extend this creative moment? Save NO for when you really need to say NO – it will retain it's impact when it is used sparingly. When we say NO to children about things like flyswatters and roller brushes it is because there is a part of us that feels we need to be the boss. We worry that we are letting them get away with something, or that they will become spoiled or demanding because they are getting their way, but please please hear me on this – we are not talking about a major ethical issue here, we are not addressing a moral dilemma – we are talking about a paintbrush!

I teach my teachers, and my workshop participants to begin saying YES as often as possible. Not YES because you are letting them get away with something. YES because YES keeps the energy flowing and keeps the explorations moving ahead in a way that allows for deeper thought and creativity.

When I was an acting student in Chicago, a large part of the training consisted of doing improv scenes where our teacher would give us a few descriptions about the situation and we were left to "do" the scene for the class. When improving dialogue you will often ask questions to keep the energy moving forward and to keep the scene alive. When asking questions of your fellow player and they said "YES," "SURE," or "OKAY" the scene stayed alive and kept moving, kept progressing, the minute a player said "NO," "NOT YET," or "NOT RIGHT NOW," it would die. One person was trying to move forward while someone was stopping it dead in its tracks.

Working with children is no different. The children are throwing out questions and requests; our answers determine the length, intensity and power of the scene that gets played out. Use that power *with* and *for* the children, not over them. Say YES as often as possible. *Go get the flyswatter!!*

Creativity Killer #5: Pressure

Lofty inappropriate expectations of a child's ability and performance can cause undue pressure and lead to frustration for both adult and child. When children are expected to "make a picture for mommy" and, on top of that, make a picture that "looks like something" when they are still in the scribble scrabble stage of creating and drawing, the child is pressured to perform above his years and ability, and forced to move through essential stages at too quick a pace.

Rhoda Kellogg identified twenty basic scribbles that serve as the starting point for not only childhood artistic creativity but for writing as well. From making basic, random scribbles on a piece of paper, the child will move onto placing these scribbles in seventeen different, yet consistent places on their paper. From here they will make shapes, then move on to combining shapes. From here we see the creation of suns, humans and then flowers. Eventually we will see rainbows, buildings and houses, and then transportation objects like cars and trucks.

In essence things that "look like something" cannot be created until the children have had the time and experience of drawing (over and over again) the lines, shapes, squiggles and scribbles they will need in order to put these things together on their paper! Houses and people are combinations of shapes. Shapes are combinations of lines and scribbles. It is only *after* being allowed to cycle through these universal stages that they combine all of their skills to make pictures containing that which we call "representational art", meaning - something that looks like something.[4]

Examples of Rhoda Kellogg's stages of scribbling have been included at the end of the chapter for your review and reference. As you look at the examples you can see how one leads to the next. We must try our best not to force them to make humans if they are still making dots. We must not suggest suns if they are still making roving lines. We must debunk the belief that child art is worthless unless it looks like something! We must realize that self-taught scribbles, lines, dots and circles constitute the beginning elements of artistic creativity. We must learn to be patient and allow children to proceed through the many stages of scribbling without a lot of undue comments and pressure.

Creativity Killer #6: Lack of Time

Children need lots and lots of free time to savor and explore an activity. We posted a sign on the door of one of my classrooms that said, "This is a child's place and we move at a child's pace." Child time is totally different than grown-up time! There is a blatant difference between the rhythms of children and the adults who spend time with them.[5] When children are interrupted and torn out of deep concentration their innate desire to work through something is compromised. Statements such as, "Hurry up!" "Time to go!" and "Come over here and do something else!" deprives children of the chance to stay with an activity for as long as it captivates their imagination.[6]

Permitting a beginning, middle and end to a play session is very important. If always pressured to, "Hurry and clean up" prior to the play being "done," the child is essentially never given time to finish. Soon these children will loose interest in starting anything because the pattern is set that there is never enough time to see it through. This then, in turn, leads to preschool classrooms filled with "bored" children who have never been permitted to explore their intrinsic interests because clocks and schedules are given more priority than the children.[7]

Adults are in a time crunch, always pressured to move on and hurry up. They unknowingly often pass this pressure on to their children. Ann Lewin, Director of the Washington DC Children's Museum states, "children are being hurried through their lives without allowing their natural rhythm to unfold. This, more than anything, will stifle their creativity."[8] Children need *time* to get involved with things that interest them. I have seen a lot of curriculum that is a mile wide and an inch deep. On the surface it looks like the children are covering so much ground, but there is no time to absorb anything. When I heard educator Alfie Kohn speak to a group of elementary teachers he too addressed the time issue.[9] He used the analogy of Americans traveling to Europe, hurry up, go here, go there, take pictures, capture it on video, no time to stop and see it, we have to catch the train by 4:45. "We'll watch it on video when we get home," they say. No time spent to enjoy the process, no time to really absorb the experience.

Time is essential as we begin to cultivate creativity.

Creativity Killer #7: Measurable Outcomes = Funding

Strong arts programs improve communication and critical thinking skills. The arts strengthen academic and social skills. These facts, according to the recent study, "Critical Links: Learning in the Arts and Student Academic and Social

Development" can in turn, aid students in learning other subjects.[10] Strong arts programs increase creativity and assist students in performing better in subjects such as literature, math, history and science. Author Robert Goldrich offers, "One explanation is that when they discover that the arts are relevant to their lives, children then see the relevance of education in other areas. They become engaged by and in the educational process." [11] Yet art and other "arts" programs, such as music and drama, are the first things cut from budgets and are missing in so many schools! In California, the late 1970's saw the passage of Proposition 13, which capped property taxes and shrank school budgets. Some critics identify this as the beginning of the end of the arts in schools as classes in music, dance, drama, drawing and painting were quickly cut. But the pendulum swings from one extreme to the next before finding a middle ground and in response to falling to the bottom rung of the "arts in education ladder," California established a task force and spent *four years* trying to determine how to get the arts back into our public schools. The final outcome? A shiny set of content standards for the arts along with a detailed list of all the things every child needs to know at every grade level about the arts. And while a mandatory arts exam is not expected anytime soon, the newly formed California Arts Assessment Network is working on ways for districts to voluntarily measure the student's expertise.[12]

"Measuring expertise" evokes images of grades… blue ribbons… assemblies… one happy person…hundreds of upset ones…Of course this "expertise" will inevitably lead to a plethora of new bumper stickers we will soon see on our roadways: "My Child was Scribbler of the Month at Yadda Yadda Preschool," "Artist of the Month on Board!" and "My Child is the Most Creative Child Ever at Such and Such Elementary" and of course, the rebellious options: "My child runs with scissors," "My child beat up your art student," will soon follow.

Why did it take *four years* to figure out how to get the arts back into schools? Why didn't anyone just go out and put an easel in every room? Buy some glue and glitter for each grade? Get some paper and paint for the children? Start a choir? Bring in a dance teacher? Start a band? *Professor Hill where are you???* [13]

Why a focus on measuring and evaluating? Maybe because adults often have an end product in mind for everything they do so for them any action not leading to that end seems to be a waste of time. Or maybe it's because, starting in 2003, all students applying for admission into the California University system will be required to have had one year of the arts during high school and the only classes that count will be those that are *aligned with the content standards.* [14]

We have a lot of work to do.

Creativity Killer #8: Baby Gap Syndrome

There are many faces to Baby Gap Syndrome[15] (BGS) – let me elaborate: meet "Little Man." Little Man suffers from BGS. He comes to school dressed to the hilt in his designer shorts and shirt. His shirt remains tucked in all day and he even wears a belt. His hair is slicked back and the gel holds it in place, he looks good, he even smells good! Little Man changes his shirt after lunch. His sneakers remain white day in and day out and he always looks neat as a pin. He also, however, does absolutely nothing all day for fear of getting messy or dirty. When he does choose to play with the playdough, he washes his hands every five minutes. Little Man cries if he gets a little bit of paint on his shirt and has an emotional breakdown on the playground when he gets mud on his new sneakers.

Then there is Little Miss. Little Miss also suffers from BGS. Little Miss dresses better than any of her teachers. Little Miss has shoes that match her Little Miss purse, she has never been seen in jeans. Little Miss often comes to school wearing party dresses that cost more than her teacher's weekly paychecks. Little Miss has a clear vision of where the bow in her hair needs to be. Like our Little Man, Little Miss tends not to be very active during the day because her clothing prevents it. When she does roll up her taffeta and get into the ooblick she will often end up in tears asking you to please "throw my dirty shirt away so mama won't get mad." At some point during the year Little Miss will bound into school announcing that she isn't allowed to paint anymore because it "ruins my clothes."

Don't you wish you had a dollar for every time you said, "Please send your child to school in clothes you don't care about!" We can encourage, demand, threaten, bribe, write notes home, scream, post signs and tell parents until we are blue in the face about the importance of wearing "play clothes" to school, but to no avail! It is frustrating to feel like our words are ignored, and even more so when, after all our efforts and insistence, the children still come to school suffering from BGS.

I have seen children proudly drag their parents out onto the yard to show off the tree forts, castles and mud houses they spent all day building and creating, designing and painting only to be asked, "Why are you so dirty?" and be informed with heavy sighs, "There's paint on your new shoes."

It makes me want to scream! What message is sent when there is so much emphasis on clothing and footwear at the expense of playing and exploring? Can the shirt really be more important than the opportunity to engage in a new creative experience? If it is, then it is a shirt that does not belong in preschool. I actually had a child come to school once wearing a green, crushed silk, flower girl dress and on her feet were tap shoes! I looked at mama, who smiled, shrugged her shoulders and said, "Well, that's what she wanted to wear! Have a good day!" Then she turned and bounced out the door. Sure, her daughter wanted to wear it, but who would get yelled at if it got covered in ooblick, flubber or easel paint?

Before I continue though, I want to stand up and tip my hat with gratitude to the parents who do realize the importance of play clothes. A big thank you to the parents who don't worry about whether or not the shirts and shorts "match" but care more about their children having a fun exciting day. Hats off to the parents who might still choose to dress their children in designer clothes but don't get hung up and bent out of shape when the logos and labels get muddy. We are able to watch your children run around and play without observing the hesitation that is so often apparent in children who have not been given this little bit of freedom.

During program orientation and back to school nights, I tell all the families, "Send them in clothes you don't care about!" I then show slides of the children in action and they immediately understand why I say this!

I met a director who tells parents, "If your child doesn't get dirty at school, then we aren't doing our job!" Another friend who provides family childcare tells all her new clients, "I guarantee I will ruin their clothes!" And a colleague who teaches preschool tells her families, "If you want the children to be able to wear it in public again, don't let them wear it here!" Sound too harsh? Too firm? Maybe. But sometimes our words need to be firm so they understand that we are serious!

The reason I like to show parents the slide show is so they can see firsthand what the children are doing and begin to understand the creative process! I have discovered that parents sometimes have a misconception that their children are getting dirty because teachers are not paying attention. Slide shows, short video clips and photographs are tools for educating parents, not only of the creative process, but also of your involvement and investment in the activity as well.

In addition, through parent workshops, parent meetings, articles about hands-on, creative messy play, a back to school orientation and well-written contracts and parent handbooks, you can begin to battle BGS. Educators and providers need to be able to verbalize why creative art and other kinds of messy play is important. We must be able to identify the skills that are being developed as children engage in these hands-on experiences. Remember that the parents aren't there during the day to see the creativity, cooperation and process first hand; all they might see is the red paint in the hair and the glue on the jeans.

In our programs children are not required to wear smocks but we do use washable paint for all projects. At orientation, parents are informed of the high level of creativity we encourage so they are asked to keep lots of extra clothes in their child's cubby. Understanding that lots of extras can be taxing for some families, there is also a big tub of community clothes I have accumulated over the years at garage sales and consignment shops that children can borrow from if necessary.

And finally, please please please make sure you are dressing the part too! One of the saddest things I've ever seen was a child running to welcome her teacher back after an absence, only to be told, as the teacher backed away from her small painty hands, "Don't touch me."

As the grown-up who is facilitating this play, whether you wear the hat of father, mother, grandparent, teacher, provider, play group monitor (or all of the above), you must also be dressed for creative play. Save the fancy clothes, the nightclub clothes and the designer clothes for locations where they are appropriate, not the preschool. Just as we expect children to come dressed ready for play, you too must follow this advice. I encourage my teachers to buy three pairs of pants they don't care about and a whole bunch of shirts from the Goodwill. No one is here for a fashion contest; we're here to be with children. If you are dressed in clothes that you are worried about you will shy away from messy, creative, child-centered play. If you back away from the art table for fear of "getting dirty" guess what the children in your class are going to do?

Please understand that I am aware of and respect the fact that certain religious belief systems dictate and regulate the clothing worn by its members. It has recently, however, come to my attention that some non-religious, community preschools are beginning to mandate their female teachers to wear dresses, nylons and heels to work. I am not aware of any clothing codes mandates for the males who are working at these establishments. However I do wonder as to how professionals who barely make a livable wage are expected to purchase this kind of clothing! Are these schools providing a clothing allowance for the required items? Does the wearing of "nice clothes" encourage (or hinder) the creative, messy, artistic, child-centered play that we know is vital to early development?

I am told that these clothing requirements are designed to promote professionalism thus encouraging parents to treat the teachers with respect. It is my belief that teachers need to be able to move around, clean up spills, change diapers, be burped on, be thrown up on, run after children, roll on the floor, play in the mud and water and provide creative art experiences each and every day. *As long as their clothing, shoes and accessories do not interfere or impede on their ability to do their job of being with children, I do not see why it matters how they are dressed.*

I expect my teachers to dress appropriately. I don't want to see body parts hanging out of clothing. I expect them to smell decent and to take pride in their appearance. At the same time it needs to be acknowledged that professionalism comes from *within* and, if truly a quality held by the teacher, will present itself daily during interactions with colleagues, parents, directors and children. Wearing socks or being barefooted, sporting heels or Birkenstocks, jeans or a suit, a tie or a t-shirt, a sport coat or overalls won't matter a bit if the teacher is there for the right reason in the first place!

You do not become a professional by wearing certain clothes. Putting a skirt on Laminated Lady would not have made her a better teacher. Professionalism is observed through someone's passion for their work and commitment to the children – not their clothing.

Twenty Basic Scribbles as identified by Rhoda Kellogg

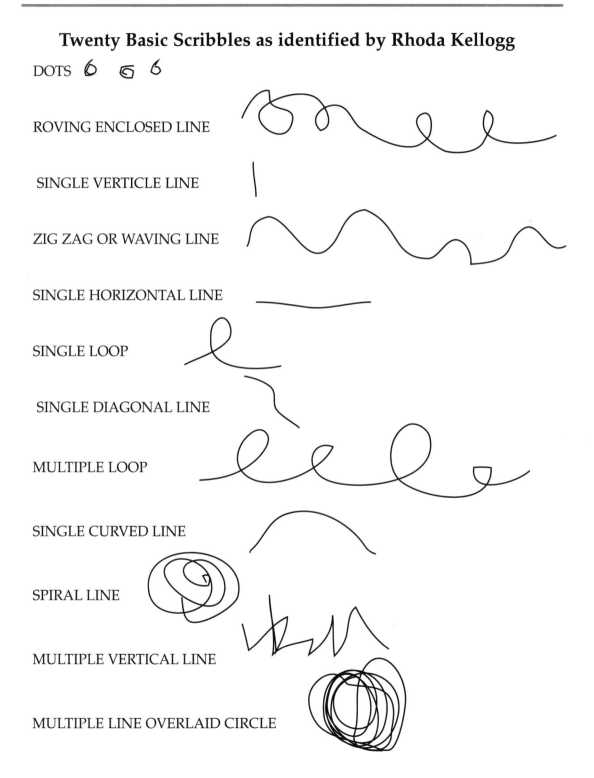

DOTS

ROVING ENCLOSED LINE

SINGLE VERTICLE LINE

ZIG ZAG OR WAVING LINE

SINGLE HORIZONTAL LINE

SINGLE LOOP

SINGLE DIAGONAL LINE

MULTIPLE LOOP

SINGLE CURVED LINE

SPIRAL LINE

MULTIPLE VERTICAL LINE

MULTIPLE LINE OVERLAID CIRCLE

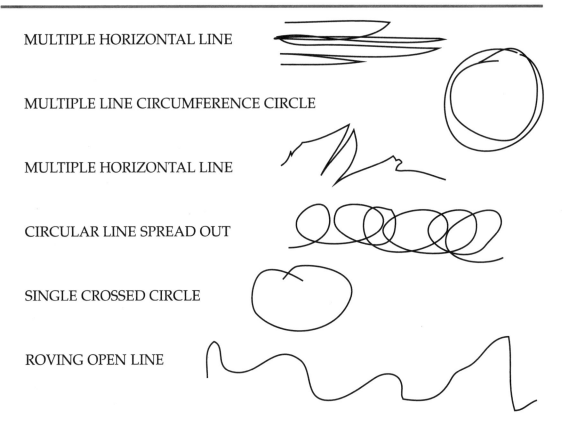

MULTIPLE HORIZONTAL LINE

MULTIPLE LINE CIRCUMFERENCE CIRCLE

MULTIPLE HORIZONTAL LINE

CIRCULAR LINE SPREAD OUT

SINGLE CROSSED CIRCLE

ROVING OPEN LINE

Following experimentation with the basic scribbles, children will begin to link what they know, create new shapes, new designs and will proceed through the following stages prior to creating representational art and prior to writing:

IMPLIED DIAGRAMS AND SHAPES   CROSSES

COMBINATIONS USING 2 SHAPES

AGGREGATES -
(3 or more shapes)

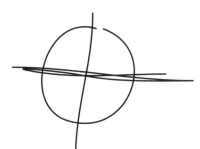

MANDALAS (Dividing space into equal parts)

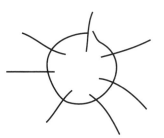

SUNS　　　　　RADIALS　　　　　SUNS WITH FACES

HUMANOIDS　　　　　HUMANS

The Importance of Creating... In Review:

1. Watch out for creativity killers.

2. Creating is NOT limited to visual arts.

3. Be aware of the stages of scribbling.

4. Realize the importance of process not product.

5. Make sure there is enough time for creative exploration.

6. Creative play can be messy play – dress accordingly.

Things to think about:

1. How do I make time for creating in school?

2. How do I make time for creating in my own life?

3. In what area(s) am I creative?

4. Have I, up until now, viewed "creativity" as being limited to the visual arts?

5. Are there children in my class who are more "non-art" creative?

6. What might they need from me to continue this level/style of creativity?

7. How can I make the environment more welcoming for them?

8. Does my school suffer from baby gap syndrome?

9. Can we make a small step toward dealing with this?

10. Which of the creativity killers do I struggle with most? Why?

11. What can I begin to do about it?

12. Which one of the creativity killers do I struggle with least? Why?

13. What is one thing I can do Monday to begin making time each day to create?

Notable and Quotable

Art is the language of the heart.

-Margaret Mead, Anthropologist

The only education worth having is an art education.

-Abraham Maslow

You can run an art program for an entire year for what it costs to buy a computer.

-Rena Upitil, *Child and the Machine*

Creativity and imagination are the keys to producing life long learners.

-Robert and Michelle Root-Bernstein, *Sparks of Genius*

Imagination is more important than knowledge.

-Albert Einstein

Chapter 2

Make time each day to...Move

Can you remember the *feel* of hopscotch, leapfrog, cartwheels, piggy back rides, playing ball, turning somersaults, climbing trees, twirling until you fell down dizzy, hopping on pogo sticks, swinging and leaping out of swing sets, spinning hula hoops, Ring Around the Rosie, Red Rover Red Rover, kick ball and jumping in and out of mud puddles?[1]

Where were you granted permission to engage in such active play? Daddy's den? The neighbor's living room? Grandma's front room? Usually not. Most of us would say that we found this freedom when we were outside in the yard, at the park and in the vacant lots where we spent hours jumping rope, riding bikes, playing tag and otherwise running ourselves silly.

A child's mind develops as a result of physical movement. Ninety-seven percent of all learning takes place from the neck down.[2] The brain is activated when the whole body is used.[3] From our knowledge of physical development we know that children grow from the neck down and from the trunk out[4] which means that the large, gross motor muscles of arms and legs need to be developed and strengthened before the fine motor muscles of hands and fingers. Large motor activities such as climbing, jumping, running and spinning come *before* small motor activities like holding pens and pencils, tying shoes and zipping zippers.

All of the above statements are easily found in any research conducted on the importance of physical movement and are readily accepted as fact in most early childhood communities. Because of this research, our challenge in making time each day for moving is not in that we need to *prove* that children need to be outside moving their bodies, our predicament is in having these beliefs accepted by our society and our culture.

The outside environment is more conducive to the active learning style of young children yet, at the time of this writing, a whopping forty-percent of the schools in the United States have eliminated recess.[5] Why? The reasons usually consist of some version of following:

- fear of lawsuits over playground injuries

- the sudden (yet questionable) increase of "unsavory adults" lurking nearby

- a shortage of adults willing to supervise the playground

- the current ever present battle cry for better academic performance

- the demand for higher test scores.[6]

In 1998 there was an elementary school in Virginia that did not have recess, instead, it had a "Walk and Talk" program[7] where, after lunch, children were allowed to walk around four orange cones that were set up in the yard. Although it was considered "social time," the children had to keep their voices down and all walk in the same direction. Three years later, after a protest led by local parent Rebecca Lamphere, not only was recess mandated by the city school district, but by the state as well.[8] During the same year, Benjamin Canada, the then superintendent of schools in Atlanta, Georgia was quoted as saying; "You don't increase test scores by having kids hanging around on the monkey bars." While Virginia was mandating recess, Georgia was taking it away. Atlanta was the first school district to eliminate recess - going so far as to build the Cleveland Avenue grammar school without a playground.[9] Due to the pressure of raising test scores, school officials often claim they have no choice but to eliminate what they consider being the "most expendable" part of the day.[10]

I find this practice completely unacceptable.

My fantasy is, of course, that each and every school board member, administrative personnel and politician who approves such outlandish doctrine as eliminating recess from our preschools in the name of "getting them ready for kindergarten" and from our elementary schools in response to "higher test scores" be required to teach these children...for a week...when it's raining. I will then inquire as to whether or not recess is still viewed as an "expendable" waste of time.

In concentrating so much on the development of their minds, we have forgotten about their bodies.[11] I am quite sure that teachers everywhere, quite specifically in Atlanta, can attest to the fact that when children are deprived of appropriate locations, such as playgrounds where they can engage in developmentally appropriate, large motor, physical feats, they begin doing them in the classroom.

Special Today: Labels Du'Jour and Acronyms A La Mode

Many teachers whose districts have traded recess time for "work time" now spend extra hours trying to "teach" when all the children actually need is a break! New educational dictates in San Diego set forth by Superintendent Alan Bersin mandate that literacy be taught in uninterrupted three-hour time blocks and math in two-hour uninterrupted blocks.[12] Upon his arrival to the district, Superintendent Bersin had full intention of completely eliminating recess. Fortunately for the children in San Diego, his wish was not granted.

Recess provides a welcomed change of pace as well as time away from formal lessons in order to socialize and relax. After a vigorous playtime students return to their classroom better able to concentrate.[13] Why then are we still seeing the elimination of the time formerly known as recess? What happens when it's gone?

Let's take a peek:

Preschoolers with limited outside time begin to run and shout in the classroom, elementary students wiggle in their desks unable to focus on the lesson at hand. This happens day in and day out. Children are told to "Sit still! Sit still!" "Pay attention!" "Eyes on me!" "Focus!" "Stop moving around!" And then the breaking point is reached, "You know, I'm *tired* of telling you to sit still!" says the teacher, "I think you must be hyper! You need an assessment!"

Labeling has commenced.

The "hyper" child is then shuffled from classroom, to principal's office, to doctor where she is given an assessment, an evaluation, an Individualized Education Plan (IEP), a diagnosis of A.D.D. (attention deficit disorder) or A.D.H.D (attention deficit hyperactivity disorder) - or sometimes both - and a prescription. And now, much to the teacher's relief, our out of control child is given medication - medication that will "assist" her in focusing, keeping still and paying attention. The magic medicine will make the child easier to handle (or is it control?) thus making the teacher's day run a little smoother.

We are very quick to write a prescription and dispense medication, yet I wonder if anyone is questioning why the student might be so wiggly in the first place? *Does anyone dare question whether or not the information she is being demanded to pay attention to is worth listening to and sitting still for?*

It is my experience that many so called "hyper kids" are really crying out for someone to pay attention to them and provide projects, assignments, activities and experiences that are meaningful and relevant. They need to get up, move around, touch things and be fully engrossed in activities. Not passively sitting at tables and in desks *watching*. Instead, they need to be *doing*.

I worry that, for whatever reason, rather than figuring out what these children need from us and from their classrooms, we simply stuff them full of medication to make them more manageable.

The psychological reference tool used for diagnosing syndromes and disorders is called the *Diagnostic and Statistical Manual*, often simply referred to as the DSM, it is currently in it's fourth edition, thus commonly called the DSM-IV. This book lists signs and symptoms of all the various psychological disorders. In addition, it presents the diagnostic criteria used by doctors to determine whether or not a patient "has" the specific disorder. From these lists of symptoms, a patient needs to have a certain number of them before a diagnosis is given. Listed here for your reference are the behaviors from the DSM-IV that would qualify a child for an A.D.D/A.D.H.D diagnosis.

Diagnostic Criteria

A. Either (1) or (2):

1. six (or more) of the following symptoms of **inattention**:

    a. often fails to give close attention to details or makes careless mistakes in schoolwork, work, or other activities

    b. often has difficulty sustaining attention in tasks or play activities

    c. often does not seem to listen when spoken to directly

    d. often does not follow through on instructions and fails to finish schoolwork, chores, or duties in the workplace (not due to oppositional behavior or failure to understand instructions)

    e. often has difficulty organizing tasks and activities

    f. often avoids, dislikes, or is reluctant to engage in tasks that require sustained mental effort (such as schoolwork or homework)

g. often loses things necessary for tasks or activities (e.g., toys, school assignments, pencils, books, or tools)

h. is often easily distracted by extraneous stimuli

i. is often forgetful in daily activities

2. six (or more) of the following symptoms of **hyperactivity-impulsivity**:

Hyperactivity

a. often fidgets with hands or feet or squirms in seat

b. often leaves seat in classroom or in other situations in which remaining seated is expected

c. often runs about or climbs excessively in situations in which it is inappropriate (in adolescents or adults, may be limited to subjective feelings of restlessness)

d. often has difficulty playing or engaging in leisure activities quietly

e. is often "on the go" or often acts as if "driven by a motor"

f. often talks excessively

Impulsivity

g. often blurts out answers before questions have been completed

h. often has difficulty awaiting turn

i. often interrupts or intrudes on others (e.g., butts into conversations or games)

In my opinion, this is nothing more than a list of irritating behaviors. If you "do" enough of them and tick off enough of the right people, they'll slap a diagnosis on you, put it in your permanent record and pump you full of Ritalin.

Now that sounds like a quality education.

I must stop and say that based on the above criteria, I am SO very much A.D.H.D. I can't sit still, I have had to learn how to focus and pay attention. I have had to learn how to stay on task. I have had to figure out a way to keep active outside of these situations so that when I must sit and pay attention I am able to do so. I am able to sit for lectures and classes because I know that I am going to get a break. I can focus on their message and their assignments because I know that I will be given time to get up, move around, walk around campus and burn off some steam. *I can focus on what needs to be done because I know at some point I am going to be able to get up and move around…*but what happens to our children who are not given such break time? The American Academy of Pediatrics estimates that 4% - 12% of all school-aged children have been diagnosed with A.D.D. or A.D.H.D.[14] Do you know what happens when they aren't permitted to move? *They get fat and they get put on meds.*

All 8.7 million of them. [15]

In California, school children are required to have 20 minutes of outside/break/recess time. In November 2002 *California Educator* ran an article about physical activity, recess and test scores. Some teachers, who did not want to be quoted, stated that their administrators considered lunch time to count towards recess time, and one principal told teachers that the time it takes for children to walk between classes each day is to be considered PE time.[16] BAM! Away goes recess time. You get your break while walking to class. And we wonder why the children are miserable, overweight and inactive.

When children are not provided with an appropriate place to run around and move the behaviors that are typically reserved for the playground begin to make their way into the classroom! All of a sudden we have this influx of "hyper" children. Are they really hyper or are they having inappropriate expectations placed on them?

Our children are being put on drugs because they can't sit still long enough to complete a stack of dittos. This is ludicrous. We are missing the forest for the trees here! The problem is not with the child – the problem is in our expectations of the child. It is not WRONG that the child can't complete the stack of dittos. It is wrong that we are expecting him to do it in the first place.

The causal agents of A.D.H.D./A.D.D. include environmental factors such as developmentally inappropriate curriculum, rigid educational systems, lack of body movement, too much TV and computer time as well as a lack of creative play.[17] A.D.D. has been referred to by some as a recent historical development, was essentially invented in the cognitive psychology laboratories of our country and given life by the American Psychiatric Association, the U.S. Department of

Education and the chemical laboratories of our pharmaceutical corporations.[18] Consequently, the vested interest is not always in the betterment of our children – but rather in the bottom line. A.D.D. and A.D.H.D is a multi-billion dollar business for pharmaceutical companies and sales are growing at a rapid 20% each year.[19] A.D.D and A.D.H.D has become a business. Don't forget that – it's a business. And it is a business of making money – not of "caring" for your child.

Do your homework before allowing someone to put your child on medication. There are millions of children on medication for A.D.D./A.D.H.D in our country. Most of them do not need to be. They simply ticked enough people off to get awarded a diagnosis.

For those of you who might be dealing with children who display some of the behaviors we listed a few pages back, please know that just because the child engages in some of those symptoms it does not automatically mean they are A.D.D! I really really want to stress that there are numerous non-medicinal ways of dealing with the behaviors that might be causing your child to be incorrectly labeled as A.D.D. or A.D.H.D.[20] A great resource book is *The Myth of the A.D.D. Child* by Dr. Thomas Armstrong. It provides 50 ways of dealing with many of the behaviors without falling into the Ritalin trap.

In addition, it is to our advantage both as parents and providers to brush up on our knowledge of Learning Styles. There are Visual Learners, who take in information about the world around them primarily through their eyes, Auditory Learners, who prefer processing new information via their ears and Kinesthetic Learners, the hands-on, learn by touching it types. It is the Kinesthetics who are often incorrectly labeled as A.D.D./A.D.H.D.

It is in our best interest (and our children's) to have a general understanding of these three basic learning styles. Why? Again – many of the children incorrectly labeled as hyper and subsequently put on medication are not A.D.D. or A.D.H.D., they are kinesthetic learners! They learn through their body! They touch everything and move around a lot because they organize information through their bodies.

Now I must interrupt with a quick sidebar here – *we are all ALL of these things.* Everyone is visual, auditory and kinesthetic. When you are reading the paper you are tapping into your visual skills, when listening to a song on the radio your auditory skills kick in and when opening a jar of mayonnaise you are using your kinesthetic abilities. See what I mean?

What you do have though, is a *preference* of how you take in information. Please please please do not think "Oh – well I'm visual so I can't listen when teacher is talking." or " I'm auditory – I can't write the essay." No no no... no labeling! No "excusing." Instead – an understanding. It is this *understanding* that will assist us – especially when it comes to working with children who have a kinesthetic preference while we would prefer them to sit and read quietly.

Visual learners organize information through their eyes. During story time these children are clamoring to be right in front of you so they can see the pictures – yet they still holler out, "I can't see!! I can't see!!" Children with a visual preference notice your first gray hair, your new purple toenail polish, your shiny new red car and even the zit that sprouted on your chin overnight. They love to read and write. They enjoy experimenting with inventive spelling. They like to use sidewalk chalk to write stories. They are list makers and need to write everything down.

Our auditory learners, on the other hand, don't need to write it down. Instead, they are asking if they can audiotape the lecture. They take in new information through their ears. During circle time they are not even on the carpet with you and the rest of the class – they are over in the block center, the sandbox or at the table coloring a picture. But what are they still doing? That's right. They are still listening to you! These children are not the "1-2-3! Your Eyes On Me" types – their *ears* are on you instead! They like to listen to music, they tend to be chatty and really enjoy talking on the phone. Visuals would rather get an e-mail. Children with an auditory preference enjoy listening to lectures and story times. As they get older they might do their homework with the stereo headset on – much to the dismay and frustration of the *visual* parent! "Take those things off! How can you concentrate!? They are so distracting!!" Distracting to whom though? The child? The parent?

Our kinesthetic learners prefer *acting out* the story, not listening to it, *doing* the science experiment, not watching it and *building* the model airplane, not reading about it in a book. They have to be up and moving. These are the children during group time who are standing in the back (you want them to sit) they are asking you questions (you want them to be quiet) they are touching everything in sight (you want them to be still). You know who I'm talking about!

Now, if you had a room full of visual learners – would you put blindfolds on them? Of course not. Would you put cotton in the ears of an auditory learner? No way. Yet every time we tell the kinesthetics to "sit still and be quiet!" we are essentially doing the same thing to them. For whatever reason the kinesthetic child falls through the cracks. I am not going to lie to you – it is easier to meet the needs of a visual or auditory learner. But we aren't after easy – we are after meaningful… it is harder to figure out what the movers and shakers need. But that's our job and we need to figure it out.

I heard about a very creative teacher who, instead of taking the easy way out and demanding testing and medications, gathered up a few milk crates and filled them with big, thick, heavy college text books. When the one of the children started getting antsy she would say, "Hey! You know – Mr. Jones needs his books back – can you get them to him please?"

With that, out goes the child, the books and the milk crate… upon arriving at Mr. Jones' room, the crate filled with books having been dragged down the hall due to sheer bulk, Mr. Jones would say, "Thanks so much! Mrs. Smith needs hers back as well." And with a nod to the corner, a second milk crate filled with even more books would be dragged back down the hall.

A 15-minute break from assignments, desks, tables and chairs and probably enough energy exerted to allow the child to come on back and stay focused on the task at hand. Maybe not as "easy" as medications, but definitely more meaningful.

So which learning style preference works best within our current, traditional, educational model? Which one does not? Which child will be sent to the office for being disruptive? Which one will receive notes sent home for not paying attention in class? Who is accused of not being on task? Who could be mistakenly labeled as having an attention deficit disorder?

I am concerned with the haste in which we are diagnosing, labeling, prescribing and medicating children. Many of the children who are said to be A.D.D. or A.D.H.D. suffer from what Dr. Thomas Armstrong refers to as "disappearing symptom syndrome." Amazingly enough their "hyperness" decreases in classrooms with engaging, interactive, supportive teachers but suddenly "appear" again when in rigid, over-controlling environments. Then, like magic, they disappear again when back in the engaging classroom![21] Not surprisingly symptoms usually disappear completely when in gym class, on the football field or while running the track. Hmmmm…

If these children truly had an organic impairment, common sense tells us that they would be displaying their symptoms all the time. Not just in certain situations. If you have heart disease, you have heart disease wherever you go. If you have polio, you have it wherever you go, not just when you are in Laminated Lady's classroom.

My personal experience is that when these "hyper" children are offered adequate outdoor playtime in addition to meaningful and interesting experiences in their indoor environments, their symptoms disappear. I am reminded of a time when I was asked by a preschool teacher to come and observe one of her students who she thought might be A.D.H.D. Upon my arrival I spoke with the director and the teacher, received some input, and then spent the morning watching the child interact with the environment, the materials, the teacher and the other students. We spent some time inside and then moved out onto the yard. As we were watching the children on the bikes, playing with sand and shovels, climbing ladders, swinging and sliding I inquired as to what the teacher's concerns were regarding the child's behavior on the playground. "Outside?" she said, "Oh, he's fine outside."

Now you see it! Now you don't!

Ritalin, a stimulant, and also the drug of choice for the treatment of hyperactivity, is classified by the Food and Drug Administration (FDA) as "highly addictive" along with amphetamines, cocaine, morphine, barbiturates and opium.[22] Children labeled A.D.D. or A.D.H.D. are often given Antidepressants such as Desipramine, Antipsychotics such as Haldol or Orap, Anticonvulsants such as Tegretol, Antianxiety Agents such as Buspar and even Blood Pressure Medication such as Clonidine.[23] These prescriptions are often given to children when really the only thing wrong is that his body is being deprived of the outside time that allows him to engage in the movement and gross motor activities he needs not only to grow and develop, but also to eventually sit still and pay attention.

EDITORIAL/LETTERS Monday, May 20, 1996 page A14

The New York Times

Whose Attention Disorder Does Ritalin Treat?

To the Editor:

Re "Boom in Ritalin Sales Raises Ethical Issues" (Health page, May 15): The stimulant Ritalin treats the needs of health professionals, parents and teachers rather than the needs of children

You report that experts say "the drug helps anyone to concentrate, whether or not they have a neurological problem." Yet you quote them as agreeing that there is a bona fide neurological syndrome, attention deficit disorder. The experts also contend that they can determine who does and who does not have this "disease."

In fact, there is no medical, neurological or psychiatric justification for the A.D.D. diagnosis. The key "symptoms" include such behavior as "often fidgets with hands or feet or squirms in seat," "often leaves seat in classroom or in other situations in which remaining seated is expected" and "often has difficulty awaiting turn."

Many factors could lead a child to behave in this manner, including a spirited, creative nature that defies conformity, inconsistent discipline or lack of unconditional love, boring and oversized classrooms, an overstressed teacher, lack of teacher attention to individual educational needs, anxiety due to abuse or neglect at home or elsewhere, conflict and communication problems in the family and misguided educational and behavioral expectations for the child.

In my own clinical experience, many such children are energetic, creative and independent youngsters struggling within the constraints of an inattentive, conflicted or stressed adult environment. Thus we end up drugging our best and our brightest.

Attention deficit disorder does not reflect children's attention deficits but our lack of attention to their needs.

PETER R. BREGGIN M.D.

Director, Center for the Study of Psychiatry and Psychology

Bethesda, Md., May 15, 1996

The Importance of Risk Taking

Climbing up rope ladders, swinging on tummies, jumping off of rocks into puddles - not only are these risk taking movements developing those essential large motor muscles, they are preparing children for reading. Risk taking encourages problem solving, critical thinking and has been identified as a fundamental prerequisite for fluent reading. Children who are afraid to risk rarely become fluent readers.[24]

Children also need the freedom to engage in appropriate risk taking movements such as: jumping off swings, swinging on their tummy, "spider swinging" (when two children face each other and swing together on the same swing), jumping off rocks, climbing structures, and rope swings. They need not be restricted from climbing up the slide or from sliding down it on their tummy. Children need to be free to twist themselves up in the swing and then let go, causing them to go round and round! They need to be able to spin so fast on the tire swing that every grown-up nearby feels the need to vomit, while the children are laughing with glee, learning about balance, motion, pendulums, cause and effect, action and reaction - basic lessons in physics! Remember - children need experiences to attach words to.

It is important that behaviors such as these are allowed on playgrounds and that the enforcement of a large number of teacher-created rules are not taking the place of the facilitation of healthy, active, large motor play. Take steps to ensure that any inside rules you have like, "no jumping," "no climbing" or "no running" do not follow the children when they head outside to play.

Once I was in a program where, after a rainstorm, the teacher bundled up her children to go on a walk. "How exciting!" I thought, "A puddle walk!" No way! Just the opposite - not only did she spend the entire duration of the walk shushing all the children, she hollered at all of them for getting wet and jumping into puddles.

Granted, when outside, some children just want to wander around, catch bugs and play handclapping games; they welcome the break from lessons and a romp in fresh air. Some children though, have more physical needs and being outside is where they can engage in them.

When we were providing family childcare I would take the children on a walk or to go to the park every day. Upon our arrival, some of the mothers at the park would grab their children and, dragging them across the parking lot to their cars would sternly instruct, "Get in the van, get in the van now!" They said this because I was known to let children climb up the slide, as well as do other outrageously dangerous things like swing on their tummies, twist up in the swings, slide down the slide face first and make wet sand for castles.

One woman in particular would never pack up and leave the park, but instead found it necessary to shake her finger at my children and constantly tell them, "NO!" "Don't!" "STOP!" and otherwise try to control the actions of everyone left at the playground. One afternoon my Dylan got on the swing and twisted it up all tight. He twisted and twisted and then he let go! He spun like crazy and became very dizzy. Of course, he did it again, and again. On the third or fourth round of swing twisting this woman approached Dylan, shook her finger and hollered, "That is not what you are supposed to do on the swings!" Dylan, almost falling over, reeling with the childhood delight of being dizzy, looked at her and said squarely, "Yeah, but I was doing physics."

I had to duck behind the rock to conceal my gales of laughter. She never shook her finger at any of the children ever again.

Children need to move around. They cannot sit still or use inside voices. They do not have walking feet. Go outside as much as possible! Make time for active movement all day long. Run around, play tag, climb things, spin, jump and remember that on those very very hot days and very very cold days you still can be moving! Don't think that you can't move one day simply because the outdoors is not available to you! Get creative! Movement happens inside too! Grab a partner, toss on a CD and get moving! Teach the children a folk dance. Remember the Macarena? Children are also able to learn an easy waltz and a two-step. I have a vivid memory from first grade when an outside "visitor" came in and taught us all the Bus Stop! *(Did I just date myself or what?!)*

In one of my classrooms we used to dance to singer songwriter Thomas Moore's "Humpty Dumpty" song at least twice a day. The children even pulled their shirts up over their heads so as to capture the "egg look" of Mr. Dumpty! Do the Hokey Pokey, play Ring Around the Rosie, dig down deep into your own childhood memory storehouse and remember what movement games you played when you were a child, then teach them to your children. Dust off that parachute, get some beanbags, and shake a leg!

I had a student one year who loved, and I mean *loved* trains. I found a CD at the library that (can you believe it?) was nothing but instrumental train sounds with whistles and a rhythmic chugga-chugga choo-choo chorus. The children moved their arms back and forth, shuffled their feet and would be trains all day long! Recently we had a parent in our program that played the bagpipes for the children so we purchased some recordings of Scottish and Irish music. The children would run in every afternoon, right before "go-home" time and demand in their pre-toddler English, "The pa-pipes Lisa!! Play the pa-pipes!" They spun and twirled and danced with glee as they danced to tin whistles and the sounds of bagpipes.

We spend hours dancing, running, jumping and hopping. We spin in circles and climb the rope ladder. We play tag, crawl on the grass and swing on our tummies. We climb up the slide, shake the parachute, do the hokey pokey and dance to the "pa-pipes". If anyone walked in and asked what we were doing, I would stand up strong and proud and tell them confidently that we were getting ready for kindergarten.

The Importance of Moving... In Review:

1. Children must move in order to learn.

2. 40% of the schools in the US have eliminated recess.

3. The three main learning styles are: visual, auditory and kinesthetic - we are all three, but we have preferences as to how we take in information.

4. Recess is not wasted time.

5. Inactivity often gives the false impression of hyperactivity.

Things to think about:

1. Does my current program make enough time for moving?

2. What is my own personal movement level? Am I an active person? Or more sedentary?

3. Might I need to modify this in some way to better meet the needs of the children in my class or program?

4. What are my personal thoughts on outside playtime and recess?

5. Where, how and what did I play when I was a child?

6. What is my personal and professional understanding of ADD/ADHD?

7. Are there children in my class who might be unfairly labeled?

8. Are there ways for me to make the environment more interesting and engaging for these particular children?

9. What is one thing I can do Monday to begin making more time each day to move?

Notable and Quotable

Movement is the door to learning.

-Paul E. Dennison, *Brain Gym*

We were conceived in motion, born in motion and we must continue to move in order to learn!

-Mary Rivkin, *The Great Outdoors*

Gotta keep movin' to keep movin' my mind!

-Dr. Bill Michaelis, San Francisco State

Attention deficit disorder does not reflect children's attention deficits but our lack of attention to their needs.

-Peter R. Breggin, M.D.

To pin down a thought, there must be movement.

-Carla Hannaford, Smart Moves: *Why Learning Is Not All In Your Head*

Chapter 3

Make time each day to...Sing

I once attended a music workshop by Tom Hunter. He began the session by asking us, "What songs do you know? Who taught them to you?"

Among many other titles, we called out: "You are my Sunshine," "Red River Valley," "When Johnny Comes Marching Home Again," "Tom Dooley," "My Bonnie," "Oh! Susanna!" and "She'll Be Coming Around the Mountain."

What songs do *you* know? Who taught them to you?

Who are you teaching them to?

I learned songs from Miss Mary, from my parents, from church and from my grandparents. My grandma sang and whistled through the house all day long. It was a family joke that no matter what phrase, comment or question anyone ever stated around grandma, she could sing a song that went with it. Show tunes were the family's specialty and friendly (ok, fierce) competitions would emerge when all were gathered together to see who could identify the most. Grandma always won. This defeat inevitably led to a mad rush to the library to check out audiotapes of movie and stage musicals so we could "brush up" for next time.

Although we never quite achieved the Norman Rockwell experience of standing around a piano, with all the cousins and relatives belting out tunes while grandpa played guitar and grandma kept time on the piano, we did sing while riding in the car and as we played around the house. Radios and record players were always on. When we were young we were exposed to a variety of music: The Beatles, Led Zeppelin, Herb Alpert, Show Tunes, Big Band not to mention my father's infatuation with Iron Butterfly's infamous "Inna-gadda-da-vida."

According to Howard Gardner, musical intelligence (one of his nine kinds of intelligences) is the first one we acquire. Musical intelligence begins while still in utero as baby is exposed to mother's heartbeat and is the last kind of "smart" we loose before we die. Have you ever taken young children singing or caroling in an old folks home? Many of our elderly parents and grandparents might not remember what they had for breakfast, the names of their children or their phone numbers, yet they know all the words to "Amazing Grace."

The only things you will remember with word-for-word accuracy from childhood are songs and rhymes.[1] In addition to simply remembering the songs from your childhood, you will be able to recall the emotional context surrounding them.[2] Leading childhood expert, Bev Bos, refers to songs as "hooks to hang a memory on." If we know that it will be *songs* that stay with them their whole life, it seems to me that it is our responsibility to insure they have something to remember.

In her inspiring article, "Don't Let the Music Stop" author Kathleen Cushman worries that "technology has stolen away our voices and robbed our children of memories."[3] When her daughter was asked to identify a "mystery tune" on the piano (Yankee Doodle) and couldn't identify it after it was played through three times, Cushman realized her family, and our culture, was faced with a crisis. She laments that night-time croonings of sleepy parents have been traded in for professionally recorded lullaby tapes and favorite songs previously sung together in the car (as out-of-pitch as they might have been) have been swapped for personal head sets and stereos.

Will the songs we remember be passed down to the next generation?

Lullabies are so much more than quiet times and cuddles in the wee hours of the night. Singing songs to children lays the groundwork for listening skills and language development and provides the roots of a literary repertoire.[4] Intellectually, we might be aware of the importance of music and its impact on the development of creativity, the producing of emotional responses, cognitive growth, language development, physical growth via dancing and moving to the music and cultivation of a positive self concept.[5] Yet some of us resist bringing singing and music into our programs because we tell ourselves, "I can't sing." I hereby give you permission to no longer worry about this! It doesn't matter! Get some tapes, learn some songs, and then sing them with the children.

Singing is not performing! This is where we get stuck. We go to a workshop, gather up some new songs and then head back to the classroom on Monday. We say, "Come on over kids! Let's sing a song!"

You are ready! You knew all the words (yesterday) — you were confident (yesterday) and now as 20 sets of wide eyes stare at you from the circle time carpet you *FREEZE!* Your throat gets tight… you get sweaty… you begin to panic… your heart is racing… you open your mouth to sing… *nothing*!

"Uh, maybe we'll put a tape on!"

Let them hear your voice. Once while walking through a parking lot I walked by a mini-van and the windows were rolled down. All I heard from the back seat was, "Mom! Mom! Put the tape back on! You are NOT singing it right!" At first I thought it was pretty funny – then I thought – OH NO! She doesn't want to hear her mama! Sing to them while you are pregnant; sing to them while they are being changed, doing dishes, taking a bath. Teach them the words. Sometimes while you are singing they are listening even though they don't want you to think they are.

I was subbing once and was singing "You Are My Sunshine" not really to anyone in particular – just to the air. One little boy came up to me and said, "Hey you! My daddy sings me that whenever he wants me to try my best!"

I don't know what it means – but yet I do not see it as my job to figure out what it means. I see it as my job to keep on singing.

So when starting out you can either dig into your memory storehouse and start by singing the songs you remember or you can figure out which songs your children already know and start with those. The trick is to subtly start filling your day with a little bit more singing and remembering to *resist the urge* to make a performance out of it! We bog ourselves down with needing to sing it right, on pitch and in key and we riddle ourselves with performance anxiety. Don't turn it into a performance – start by singing to the air.[6] How? Pick one song that you know and start singing it when you are in the car, folding laundry, waiting in line at the store, when you hear a baby crying, preparing meals, giving the children a bath… no pressure, no performance, just a song. A song for you and a song for your children. The song will become a hook for your family to hang a memory on.[7]

The belief of thinking we can't sing has only emerged in the last few decades and it has coincided with the rising popularity of commercial, studio-enhanced recorded music.[8] But when we leave singing to the professionals we loose the power of our own voice. As adults we often fail to realize that infants and young children do not judge the quality of a parent's or teacher's voice by professional standards. They aren't concerned about the sound, but rather with the attention and love they are receiving.[9]

Singing and music are forms of communication. Infants are singing and communicating when they coo and say "la-la, la-la," when they are playing call-and-response games with parents and providers, when they are blowing raspberries and babies are rocked to sleep by the soothing lullabies sung by loving caretakers. Toddlers and Preschoolers learn nursery rhymes and simple songs like "Itsy Bitsy Spider" that have finger signs to go along with the words. Chanting becomes popular as do echo songs such as Ella Jenkins' popular, "Did you Feed My Cow?"

Children play with sounds by banging on drums, pots and pans and shaking tambourines and pounding the xylophone. On the back fence of our yard we hung washboards, pie tines, tin cans, hubcaps and many other sound producing objects for the children to tap, bang and otherwise "make music" on. Our environment is filled with items such as rhythm sticks, bells, drums, tambourines, pots and pans and wooden spoons in addition to the collection of handmade African instruments that my husband has chosen to share with the children. We have rain sticks, tambourines, gourds filled with beans and even film canisters filled with pebbles and sand for shaking.

When funds are available we invest in good, quality musical recordings. When they aren't we borrow from the library. We have a tape and CD player and even a record player! There was a time when the record player was only hauled down off the top shelf from the materials cabinet whenever we were going to do record player spin art. But one day I wanted to play a song from a real vinyl album for the children to hear. I slowly pulled it out of the sleeve while the children watched with anticipation. As I took it out of the jacket and held it up carefully by the edges (weren't we all taught that?) Katie stood up and announced to the class, "We have those at home, but ours are small and shiny!"

In addition to suddenly feeling old, I realized, in one brief instant, that none of the children in front of me would have memories of saving money for 45s and 33s, no late night slumber parties spent watching the album spin around and around, no lessons on learning how to be careful with the needle or the proper way of holding the album by its edges and no frustrating moments of dealing with the "skips." Instead, a world of compact disc players, Walkmans and personal stereo systems would make up their childhood musical experience. Now, not only do we keep the record player in the classroom all the time, we also make time to listen to things that are not so small, and certainly not shiny!

Once I had the experience of shadowing a four year old who was attending a preschool near my home. He had no speech. The child had been through a whole gamut of tests, assessments and ear exams, only to discover nothing. I do not necessarily jump to the conclusion that something is "wrong" when children do not speak. Sometimes, yes, there can be hearing issues, maybe a language delay. Sometimes it is a power struggle. Sometimes children just don't have anything to say to us yet. Sometimes they talk at school and not at home or vice versa. In this case the parents, teacher and director called me in mostly as an extra set of eyes, ears and hands, to see if someone in a more objective position could shed some insight. I agreed to come on site twice a week to work with him.

As I have stated many times already – children need experiences to attach words to. So the first thing I did was offer a lot of time to explore mud, sand and water. It is my experience that these raw materials serve as a great entry point into the realm of play and often language development progresses from early experiences with these basic materials ("My shovel!" "Look at this!" "I want a bucket," ect.).

From here we began to explore the yard and increase his level of physical activity. With the assumption that language springboards off of the experiences a child has, we continued to look and search for his "back door." What did he need from this place that he was not receiving? So while we played in the water, offered trucks, built with blocks and squished with clay - we punctuated each "experience" with a turn on the swings and song. He sat on my lap and we would swing, as I would sing, "My Bonnie lies over the ocean… My Bonnie lies over the sea…" This was our ritual, swinging and singing, back and forth, "My Bonnie lies over the ocean… My Bonnie lies over the sea…"

After many weeks he acquired a few words, "water," "mommy," "daddy" and "cookie." I wondered on my last day with him if I really had made an impact – only four words? What could I have done differently? When it was time to go I gave him a hug and kiss, told him I would miss him and went to my car. That night one of the teachers called me at home and said that as soon as I drove away he went to the swings, hopped on and sang out in a loud four-year old style, "My Bonnie lies over the ocean… My Bonnie lies over the sea…"

Two weeks later he started talking.

We found his back door and it was music.

Making it Meaningful

Yes, music significantly contributes to the child's social, emotional, intellectual and physical growth, but often children are exposed only to trite children's music that does nothing more than superficially entertain.[10] Instead of "cute" children's music try Duke Ellington, a Bach concerto or how about a Sousa March?! Real music and real songs are so much more significant and satisfying than educationally contrived march-like songs about tooth brushing, traffic lights or the days of the week; especially the ones sung to the tune of "Jingle Bells," "Row, Row, Row Your Boat" and "London Bridge."[11]   There are a million unsung songs lying around, waiting to be sung which are ten times deeper and lots more meaningful than songs like these.[12] Sing them.

Early in my career I was encouraged by leading educator, author and recording artist, Bev Bos, to stop singing songs that *teach*, and instead sing the songs that *include*. Up until learning this from her, I was guilty of singing the hundreds of silly, cutesy songs that all had the same tune. It was she who encouraged me to sing to the air and taught me songs that encouraged the children to actively participate by hollering out words and phrases and suggestions, songs such as "Uncle Jesse," where the children holler out what *they think* Uncle Jesse is wearing as he comes through the field. "Rainbow 'Round Me" where children say what *they see* outside of their window and "The Pirate Song" where children say what *they did* on the day they jumped aboard the pirate ship. Learn songs that encourage active participation and involvement from the children and sing them. Seize every opportunity to sing with your children! The effort and time expended is small, but the reward is so great.[13]

I taught in one school where the only singing that ever really went on was on Friday when the self-professed "Music Man" would come into the preschool, set up all his equipment, and then proceed to sing *at, to* and *for* the children, never really *with* them. He had shiny instruments and a keyboard that no one was allowed to touch. Children would holler out a song request, (always while he was singing of course) to which he'd respond, "Not right now – right now we're singing about the days of the week – come on! Join me! We all know the words!"

I so wanted to unplug his amp. I threatened a boycott. I wrote a letter to the administration. They told me I could be excused from the Music Man but that it was providing an enrichment experience for the children. A WHAT??

Please don't save songs for assemblies and holidays. Sing them now; sing them in the bathroom, in the shower, in the tub, in the rain, in the kitchen and in the car! Sing them quiet, sing them loud, tap out patterns on your legs, on pots and pans and on the steering wheel. I actually met my husband while I was "playing" a 5-gallon waterbottle like a drum while singing at a party... Tap glass jars filled with varying levels of water and listen to the sound differences. Use wooden spoons to bang on the hubcaps you find on the side of the road. Chant. Locate a Tibetan singing bowl, sing, make music and include the children.

Not sure of where to start? I have included a short list of "favorite songs" at the end of this chapter to get you off and running - but until then - do you like the Beatles? Put them on! Classical? Turn up the Mozart! Is country more your style? Bring it on! We played bagpipe music every afternoon, (the neighbors just couldn't wait), but the children were so visually moved by the experience, how could you turn it off? You could see the light in their eyes and almost see the music getting under their skin and affecting their bodies. Sing because it allows you to express yourself, sing to convey ideas and express your moods. Sing for the sheer enjoyment of it.

If you don't know the words, go to the library and get some tapes so you can learn the words, or, better yet, find someone who does and ask them to teach you. Use tapes and CDs to provide renditions of the songs, not as substitutes for singing them out loud. Don't be taken off guard if the version on a tape or CD is different than the way you sing it as many songs have folk music origins and many different renditions have been recorded over the years. Don't think that your way is wrong because it's different than the one on the tape! Be sure to have music in the background during the school day, put in tapes and songs for children to hear and dance to, just don't get stuck there and forget the impact of singing around the carpet, singing under the tree, singing around a fire and singing to the air.

I encourage you to go back and remember the songs and music of your childhood experience. What do you remember? Hand-clapping games? Jump rope songs? Church songs? Instruments? Radios? Those little 45s? The bulky 8-Tracks? It's time to tap back into the power of music and provide it for our children. And it is not as hard as we might think! Sing in the shower, while doing dishes, while cleaning the house and driving across country or when walking to the market. Sing out loud, sing with the dog, sing with your family and sing with the children. Teach them the songs, the words and the melodies of their history and their culture.

If we know that music is the first intelligence acquired and the last one we loose, it is our job to provide them with that which they will remember.

SOME SONGS TO GET YOU STARTED

Alouette (If you love me, tell me that you love me)

Are You Sleeping? (Frere Jacques)

Did You Feed My Cow?

Go Tell Aunt Rhody

Grandfather's Clock

Happy Birthday

I'm A Little Tea Pot

In and Out The Window

Mary Had a Little Lamb

Muffin Man

My Bonnie Lies Over the Ocean

Oh! Susanna!

Rainbow 'Round Me

Red River Valley

Skip to My Lou

This Old Man

Twinkle Twinkle Little Star

Uncle Jesse

Yankee Doodle

You Are My Sunshine

The Importance of Singing... In Review:

1. Sing to the air! It doesn't need to be a performance.

2. You do not need to "know how to sing" to start singing.

3. Songs are "hooks to hang a memory on."

4. You will remember all the songs you learned from your childhood.

5. Musical intelligence is the first acquired and the last to go.

Things to think about

1. Are we singing enough?

2. Do my worries about the quality of my voice get in the way?

3. What songs do I know?

4. Who can I teach them to?

5. What was my childhood experience with music, singing and songs?

6. How is that influencing (whether positive or negative) the school environment?

7. Does my classroom provide enough opportunities for making music?

8. Do we have a collection of tapes and CDs for both teacher and child use?

9. What song will I first use to begin singing to the air?

10. Have I been guilty of singing everything to the tune of "London Bridge?"

11. Do any of our clients or families have musical talents or songs they'd be willing to bring in and share?

12. What is one thing I can do Monday to begin making more time each day to sing?

Notable and Quotable

Children's music often does nothing more than superficially entertain the young.

– Marvin Greenberg, *Your Children Need Music*

I've never found anything more powerful than music to begin to heal and transform every aspect of people's lives.

-Mitchell Gaynor, M.D., *Sounds of Healing*

I would never sing a song with children that I wouldn't also sing with adults.

-Bev Bos

Violence in our time stems from not teaching music to the young.

-Polybius, 2BCE

Chapter 4

Make time each day to...Discuss

In order to learn language, children need to talk with people.[1] By talking and listening to others we learn how to organize our thoughts, communicate with others, problem-solve and develop socialization skills.[2] Children ask questions, ramble on, tell elaborate stories, and may appear to talk incessantly! Many of us have experienced the frustration that comes with the twenty-fifth, *"Mommy, how..." "Daddy what..??"* or *"Teacher, why...??"* Children continually want to discuss their world and all their new discoveries, out loud. It is not until around the age of seven when children develop what we might refer to as "inner speech" or "self talk."[3] Prior to this, children quite literally think out loud.

Until around the age of seven or eight, children can sit around on a carpet in the middle of their classroom reading aloud to themselves (or each other) and the only person who would be distracted by the whole event will more than likely be the teacher.

The need for talking out loud and hearing one's own voice is so great that some experts feel that silent independent reading is essentially ineffective until approximately age seven![4] Around this time the children learn how to internalize language in order to figure out what they want to say before saying it out loud. This process allows them to "hear" what they want to say in their mind before actually saying it; this is called the "prelude to the ability to engage in rational thought."[5]

Talking is essential to language development and to thinking. When children are given the opportunity to talk things through and verbally process new ideas with other children and with grown-ups, these thoughts become anchored in understanding yet the willingness to facilitate such verbal processing often decreases with the child's entrance into elementary school.[6]

Children working in groups, sharing ideas and solving problems together are often viewed as noisy, chaotic interruptions to the school day. Sometimes such behavior is mistakenly called "cheating." Yet we know children process information more effectively when allowed to move around and talk out loud.

A stern verbal command to, "Sit down and be quiet!" is really quite inappropriate. Why? It stops, dead in its tracks, three major experiences young children must be able to have: moving around, touching stuff and talking. What kind of learning is going on when everything is put away? When everyone is sitting still? When everything is quiet? They need to be moving through their environment, manipulating materials, problem solving and asking questions and they are not able to do this when sitting still and keeping quiet is the only real priority.

I have complied a brief list of what I call "Discussion Destroyers." These are ways we sometimes hinder problem solving and discussion with our children without even realizing it. *I was guilty of doing all of them for a long time.* Remember though that they are nothing more than habits! And with time and commitment, habits can be broken. Here's what I did:

• First, I became aware of behaviors I was engaged in

• Second, I decided that I didn't want to do them anymore

• Third, I was very patient with myself

• Fourth (save for when you are further down the journey), I audiotaped myself with the children so I could listen to how I spoke to/with them

Oh boy! What an eye opener! This last one here is what really helped me break the Discussion Destroyer habit! Do not - I repeat – do not do it right out the gate unless you are really ready to start working! We are sometimes not even aware of the language we use through the day! Taping yourself will jumpstart your self-investigation process!

It is important to remember that most of us don't engage in the Discussion Destroyers on purpose or to be malicious. We do them because we don't know any better. Until we stop to think there might be a different way of doing things, we do it the way we know how. I decided to change my mind; I give you permission to take the time to do the same.

Discussion Destroyer #1

Asking a child a question you already know the answer to

When you see a child drip yellow and blue food coloring onto white shaving cream and then use a craft stick to mix it up and make green, interrupting her experiment by asking, "What colors did you use?" is not engaging her in a discussion. It is a test to see if she knows her colors. It is searching to find what she "learned," instead of celebrating the process and discovery of making green.

A more appropriate response, if it was determined that one was actually necessary for the benefit of the child (not the adult) is, "Do you need anything else?" or "Look at that!" or possibly, "What else can I get for you?" Most of the time though, I find that a supportive, encouraging *nonverbal gesture*, such as moving the can of shaving cream closer within reach, is all the adult interaction that's really necessary.

Discussion Destroyer #2

Disregarding a child's answer to a question because you were hunting for the "right" answer

I once watched a teacher sit in front of the calendar during group time and work her way around the circle asking each child, "What day is today?" In addition to being a question she already knew the answer to, she was on the prowl for the right answer to boot. Of course, being three, four and five years old, *everyone* had a response and *everyone* wanted a turn to share. Their answers ranged from, "It's the weekend!" to, "Yesterday!" to "It's my birthday" (it wasn't) to "Morning!" Of course none were "correct" but the teacher was waiting for the "right" answer. She spent ten minutes saying, "Nooo, Noooo, Nooo," "Not really," "Ok, yes, but nooo," until, *finally*, Jenny said, "It's Friday!"

Teacher beamed at Jenny. Everyone else was silent. Then, as if on cue, it became apparent that *everyone* now had something to say about *Fridays*. There were comments about how Friday was "go-home" day and they needed to bring their nap sheets home, there were cheerful announcements of how dad visits on Friday, someone said they always get pizza and a movie for Friday and then someone announced that *next Friday* (of course) he was going to take a trip to grandpa's house to see the new puppy! This of course prompted a well-timed comment from Jeannie who had just gotten a puppy for her *birthday*, which of course turned into a group inquiry of "How many days until *my* birthday?"

And right in the middle of all this wonderful dialogue the children were hushed and shushed because now it was time to sing the days of the week song, which of course, was to the tune of "Alouette."

Talking about *it* (whatever *it* may be) is facilitating the ability to put thoughts into words, encouraging communication skills and even developing awareness of others outside of the self as the children listen to the stories and tales of others. Discussing *it* assists children in language development, exposes them to new words and experiences, allows them to use their imagination and they create mental pictures to attach to someone else's story and all sorts of other goodness that doesn't always have it's own 20 minute time block on the posted schedule.

Schedules do not make time for these important happenings – we do.

Discussion Destroyer #3

Anytime you say, "Someone already said that"

When involved in something that encourages the children to provide you with responses, such as singing songs where the children supply some of the words, never ever say, "Someone already said that." Here's why: Children are egocentric and, as the center of their own universe, they are often completely unaware of the other children around them. When you are singing "Here comes Uncle Jesse, he's runnin' through the field… with his horse and buggy and he knows just how you feel. He's hollerin' _____" (children fill in the blank here) and Mark shouts out that Uncle Jesse's hollerin' "RED PANTS!" you *know* that not two verses later someone else is going to shout out the same thing!

Although tempting to think these preschoolers are intentionally trying to get your goat, it's more probable that the second child didn't hear Mark say it first! And even if she did - so what! Sing it again!

Try with all your might to resist the urge to say, "Someone already said Red Pants."

Discussion Destroyer #4

Asking children simple "yes" "no" questions

Avoid superficial and simplistic yes-no questions by asking meaningful open-ended questions or making invitations that promote thought and discussion. The invitation to, "Tell me about your weekend" will solicit a more thoughtful response than, "Did you have fun this weekend?"

When you encourage deeper thinking and meaningful discussions through the kinds of questions you are asking, the children will come to value more meaningful conversations too.

Discussing Leads to Problem Solving

Contrary to popular belief, children do not talk all day to drive us crazy. They are processing their observations and their experiences. By encouraging and facilitating discussions we assist them as they continue to learn about and understand their world. It is therefore very important that we use descriptive language when speaking with children. Enthusiastically pointing out the *"fat red robin* that is *perched* on the wooden fence"* provides so much more than, "look at the bird."

Talking throughout the day and thinking out loud also models the process of being able to identify a problem, think about a solution, make a plan and take action. It models impulse control and the power of thinking something through instead of simply acting out in reaction to something. For example: "We are all out of chicken, so I'm going to cook macaroni for lunch today." Or, "Oh dear, we are all out of yellow paint, I hadn't noticed that yesterday. Shall we use blue instead?"

I call this, "putting your self-talk on speakerphone." I have found it is a beneficial process for everyone, not just the children. It encourages me to be patient and thoughtful as well as mindful of my actions; and it encourages me to stay in the present moment, which is very important when working with children. By watching me think out loud the children are able to observe the problem solving process in action. We are modeling the skills we want them to develop. By including them in the process we are increasing communication and socialization skills.

Learning how to communicate with others is a skill that remains long after cubby tags have faded and the preschool art has disintegrated in the boxes in the attic. Young children can easily acquire the skills needed for effective problem solving when the adults in their world are **consistent, patient, committed** and when, of course, they use good communication skills themselves! Children will do what we do. I was told once, "If you want them to do it – do it. If you don't want them to do it – don't do it." Actions *do* speak louder than words. We cannot develop effective problem solving skills in children if we cannot do it ourselves.

You must take ownership of the process of teaching problem solving skills. It is of utmost importance that our children are not simply tossed back into the middle of a playground battle over shovels and bikes with a flip comment such as, "Go use your words." What "words" do you want them to use? I know some of the "words" little children know and, like you, have witnessed Karen demanding her f---ing shovel back! while Cassie announces, "D--- it! That's mine!"

Have you taught them the proper words? Have you modeled the problem solving techniques? Unless you have given them appropriate tools you might not like what some of them are going to say.

In our programs we teach our children how to make requests of each other. A simple, "I want a turn when you're done" from one child to another is how bikes are traded and turns monitored. Teachers do not get in the middle, count laps, mandate sharing, set timers or in any other way interfere with the process of Colin figuring out how to ask Hannah for a turn on the bike when she's done. We instead teach and model so Colin learns how to do it. This takes time.

Sometimes you have the benefit of having children in your programs from the time they are infants, thus they grow up in environments that model this effective behavior. *When older children join your program it is of utmost importance that they are modeled the same skills as the other children.* Some of them will have had a previous preschool experience, some will not. We must not assume that these children come to us with an understanding of problem solving simply because they are older.

Children do not learn how to get a turn on the bike after one "lesson" or a one time modeling of how to do it. It requires the adults to be patient and consistent. Older children who have not yet been taught problem solving skills can learn them. Grown ups can learn them too, it just takes a little longer. Please know it is never too late.

The same process is true for teaching children how to speak out when they feel they have been harmed or wronged. "So-and-So took Such-and-Such's shovel," "I had it first," "He took it, it's mine!" Typical preschool politics. First and foremost, we do not allow children to be victims. If someone gets hit on the playground or in the classroom, the first thing we do is encourage the child who got hit to holler something like, "No!" "Stop!" or "I don't like that!" We teach them over and over again how to use a BIG VOICE when saying "NO!" not a little whiny one. We encourage them to find the power in themselves and in their voice as they learn how to solve their problems. We do not pay a lot of attention to the child who did the hitting. This removes the power from the act of hitting and also deflates the possibility of receiving negative attention, which some children crave.

Along with hitting and toy taking, tattling is another natural by-product of having a large number of children interacting with each other over any amount of time. Again, it is not fair to toss the child back into the drama with a simple, "Go tell *Nancy* you want your doll back" when you have not, up to that point, taught or modeled the skills necessary to do so. One of the main goals in our programs is to make sure the children are taught the words they need to go and get their doll back.

The children know from both verbal and non-verbal cues that the teacher is there to help when needed. The teacher will walk back over to the other child with them and even assist in the coaching of the dialogue. Teachers are engaged, involved, modeling and assisting children as they learn how to solve their problems. Our ultimate goal is for the children to be able to communicate successfully with others by themselves. Independently. Without needing to constantly rely on the grown-up to assist them as they solve basic problems and have day-to-day interactions with their peers.

There are also times along the way when you just need to back off and trust that the children can begin to handle things for themselves. When there is no immediate danger it is sometimes best to let children play alone without a lot of grown-up meddling and interfering.[7] Some children spend *ten hours a day* together every single day of the week. I have learned that if I get involved with every single minor incident every hour of every minute of every day *we would all go nuts.* Imagine if your mother got involved *every single time* you and your siblings or cousins or the neighbor kids had a conflict!

You would never have had the chance to practice what she had taught you. As the teacher and parent we are constantly providing skills and modeling appropriate behaviors – sometimes it is necessary to stand close by and determine if we are teaching the right ones. We are entrusted with teaching a skill that will have a life-long impact. It is important to sometimes step back and assess our progress. Anna Quindlen stated, "Each day we move a little closer to the sidelines of their lives, which is where we belong if we do our job right."

But What Are They Learning???

When preschool programs toss the importance of social and emotional skill development out the window in exchange for more rigorous, academic, technological, preparatory skill development they are depriving children of skills necessary for their future social and academic success. In "Set For Success," an in-depth report released in 2002 by the Kaufman Early Education Exchange, researchers summarized how social and emotional competence sets the foundation for school readiness. "Children entering school with well-developed social skills are most likely to succeed and least likely to need costly intervention services later through special education or juvenile justice... strong social-emotional development underlies all later growth and development." [8]

This timely report reiterates that social-emotional development and academic achievement are not separate priorities, but rather, the two work together to strengthen our children's chance of later school success. The report stresses that social and emotional well-being must be a priority if our goal is to have children entering school ready to learn and succeed.

The report continues by saying, "There is a growing realization that achieving the goal of children entering kindergarden ready to learn will require more than increased cognitive stimulation. In fact, school readiness appears to be intimately tied with social-emotional development." [9]

Again though, our struggle is not with understanding this, but in getting the general public and society to accept it! Case in point - at some point in our career we came across that one child who, at the young age of three, four or five, could identify the letters of the alphabet, play the violin, dance for grandpa, knew all her shapes, could recite her address and could count to 100 – and could do it all in six different languages. *However,* when someone took her shovel on the playground she would fall apart into a blubbering mess...Meltdown! Whining and crying she would burst up to teacher, wailing about her missing shovel, hollering and carrying on. Yes, she might be able to write her name, program the VCR and maneuver her way around the Internet, but guess what? *She doesn't know how to get her shovel back.*

And *children* who do not learn how to problem solve, discuss conflict or communicate with others, turn into *grown-ups* who can't do it either. Whiny lamentations over swiped toys, missed turns and who is looking at who, turn into even still more annoying cries about stolen parking spots, lost staplers, missing files, unfair deadlines and selfish co-workers.

It's no surprise that most adults who get fired from their jobs do not get fired because they can't do their work; but rather because they can't deal with bosses, co-workers, staff, customers and supervisors.[10] They might be able to write computer programs but they are still lacking in social ability and communication skills because they never learned how to get their shovels, err, I mean staplers, back.

Parallel this to an early childhood environment - do children get kicked out of preschool for not knowing the ABCs or 123s? Are they given the boot if they can't tie their shoes or recite their phone number? Of course not! But many are asked to leave the program if they are constantly hitting, biting, kicking and scratching - all of which indicate an absence of problem solving capabilities and a lack of social skills.

Many educators agree that social competence is more important for school success than coming to kindergarten knowing the ABC's.

When I was doing family childcare I received a phone call from a woman who had heard about our program. She was looking for a preschool for her daughter and asked me to describe what we offer. I jumped into my energetic description of our play based, hands-on and hands-in, child-centered environment and was just about to tell her of the activities taking place that particular day when she stopped me with a heavy sigh, "Ohhhh," she said, "You're one of those 'social emotional' preschools." "Umm… yes.." I said. She proceeded to inform me that her *neighbors* told her that if she put her daughter in a "social emotional" preschool she would never be ready for kindergarten. Her *neighbors??*

I gently told her that, in actuality, a social emotional preschool is really the only kind of program that prepares children for kindergarten. I shared with her that we have piles of research that confirm the fact that the only children who benefit (long term) from an early preschool experience are children who had been in child-centered, play-based, social emotional programs. I was on a roll, the soapbox had been placed on the floor and I was proudly taking my place upon it! "Come see us!" I encouraged (or was it begged?) "Come observe! Watch what we do and let your child have a go at it! What we are doing *is* kindergarten readiness – it just looks a little different than what your *neighbors* have in mind. Sometimes it's best to see it in action before making a decision!"

She stopped me mid sentence and informed me that she just couldn't "take the risk of her not being ready." Then she hung up.

I stepped off my box discouraged, mad, angry, sad and frustrated – I wanted to kick it across the room!

An Important Sidebar

In 1995 Susan Black released a summary of the work of Dr. Rebecca Marcon who had completed a study of various preschool programs and the impact they had on later school success.[11] Black tells readers how Marcon's research reveals that children who spend their preschool years in child-initiated preschools (preschools where teachers encourage children to choose and develop their own learning and where social and emotional needs are considered more important than academics) benefit more (in both the long and short term) from their early school experience than their academic oriented counterparts. Black reports that Marcon discovered that children who had been in academic preschools fell behind academically once reaching elementary grades. In addition, they lagged behind their peers in social development and by fourth and fifth grades, the children who had been in academic preschools were earning lower grades and displaying maladaptive behavior such as hyperactivity, depression, anxiety and defiance.

Then a report released in September of 2000 finally gave credibility to something early childhood educators had been saying for years – preschoolers are better off concentrating on developing their social and emotional competence than learning the ABCs and 123s.[12] It pointed out that children who do not begin kindergarten with strong social and emotional skills could often be plagued by behavioral, emotional, academic and social development problems that follow them into adulthood. The report also suggests that parents can increase a child's chance of success in Kindergarten by fostering confidence, curiosity, motivation, cooperation and (emphasis added) *the ability to communicate.*

In the book, *The Creative Spirit*, we read, "Hothouse training regimes that force math, reading and writing before children have any real interest in doing these things are not only inappropriate, but often lead to an aversion of and to the subject being taught."[13] Educator Alfie Kohn has elaborated on this point by saying, "When something is forced down our throats, it has nowhere to go but back up."[14]

Just Because They Can Doesn't Mean They Should

Here is what I know – I know that we all want what is best for our children. Here is what else I know – often times what is being sold to you as best, is not.

I met a man who teaches toddlers how to read. He sees it as providing a service. I see it more as a trap. A trap that catches well-meaning parents and makes them think that by *not* teaching their babies how to read they are somehow providing a disservice for their children.

In actuality, it is the complete opposite.

Beware of anyone who ever says anything to you like: "Oh if your child doesn't _____ by the time he is _____ he will never succeed!" Or "College choices hinge on their performance NOW!"

If you look deep enough, folks who say this kind of stuff to you are ultimately selling something. By preying on your emotions they will try to get you to buy their product. They do NOT have a vested interest in your child and his or her ultimate success. They simply want your VISA number. But because of our desire to provide for our children and do what we think is "best" (or what we are being sold as best) we fall easy suckers to their medicine show and buy their "Do it Quick! Do it NOW" program and the "Bigger! Better! Faster!" kit that they are selling from their carpetbag.

We think we are doing what is best. Everyone else is buying it... the neighbor kids all have one... The 5 o'clock news said it is what the best and brightest are using to "get ready"... You have a few questions - but the medicine show has already left, and so has your money. You look at the stuff left in exchange for your cash and you can't help but wonder, "Will it help? Will it work?"

Meanwhile, the young children are standing by twisting and pulling their hair. Their nails are gnawed down to the nubs...but they can count to 100 in three languages, can spell their names and know their shapes and colors.

Just how far are we willing to go to secure their place in the dog and pony show?

What are we sacrificing?

When will it stop?

It's So Much More Than A Catchy Phrase!

- *Down With Dittos!*

- *Sooner is not better!*

- *Childhood is a journey, not a race!*

- *Education is not the filling of a bucket – it is the lighting of a fire!*

- *Too much, too fast, too soon is not the answer!*

- *Children learn through play!*

- *Preschool is not boot camp for kindergarten!*

Battle cries such as these take the form of bumper stickers, T-shirts, key chains and buttons that we plaster all over our cars, bodies and backpacks. But, just as "discussing" makes up a vital part of our children's foundation, it plays an important role in our jobs as well. Catchy slogans are not enough.

As teachers, providers and educators, we have a professional responsibility to be able to go deeper than the bumper stickers, T-shirts and buttons. We must develop the ability to discuss and communicate our understanding of the research and the knowledge that supports hands-on, child-centered places with colleagues, parents, clients and administrators. We are then able to support that while "playing" with water, cotton balls and eyedroppers children are learning about absorption. When jumping off rocks, they are learning about gravity. When mixing cornstarch and water they experience a suspension and create a non-Newtonian fluid. When blowing bubbles they are exposed to the concept of surface tension. While "just scribbling" and painting on huge sheets of paper they are mastering spatial representation and when they dump vinegar onto baking soda they are learning about action, reaction, and the properties of carbon dioxide.

There's more to creating a high quality program than having the right equipment and an informational brochure that says you emphasize social and emotional development. Educators must be able to call upon the research that supports their classroom practice. Kathleen Glascott tells us, "If teachers can't describe the research on early childhood education – especially the research that says children learn as they play – it's likely their efforts won't be taken seriously."[15] When we are able to use research as well as anecdotal evidence while discussing our methods, we appear professional, confident and credible while making positive inroads towards the modification of what is expected at many preschools.

We know how to get our shovels back.

The Importance of Discussing... In Review:

1. Be aware of the Discussion Destroyers.

2. Discussing = Problem Solving = *learning how to get your shovel back!* And this is more important for school success than ABCs and 123s.

3. Do not be swayed by product pushers who are selling you something and really aren't vested in the true success of your child(ren).

4. Teaching problem solving takes commitment, time and patience on the part of all grown ups involved.

5. Educators have the responsibility to be able to discuss and articulate the "learning" that can be linked with the play-based experiences being provided for the children.

Some things to think about

1. How does my program make time for open-ended discussions?

2. Do I struggle with problem solving skills in my own life?

3. How do I currently assist my children in problem solving?

4. What might I need to do differently?

5. What is my comfort level with allowing children to sometimes figure things out for themselves?

6. Do I sometimes currently send them off to "use their words?"

7. How is my level of "descriptive word" usage?

8. Do I find myself often trapped by Discussion Destroyers?

9. Which one(s)?

10. Up until now did I see the link between discussing, social skills and school success?

11. How can this information benefit my program?

12. Does some of this information need to be passed on to the parents and teachers in my program?

13. When can that happen?

14. What is one thing I can do Monday to begin making more time each day to discuss?

Notable and Quotable

If you want to have intelligent conversations with children, give
your own assumptions a rest, put on your listening ears and hear
what the child is really saying.

-Jane Healy, *Creating Intelligent Conversations with your Children*

Parents can improve a child's chances of success in kindergarten
by fostering a strong relationship that enhances confidence, independence,
curiosity, motivation, persistence, self-control, cooperation, empathy,
and the *ability to communicate.*

-*Chicago Tribune*, September 6, 2000

Teaching children how to talk means teaching children how to think.

-Jane Healy

Sitting still and being quiet is not a marketable job skill.

-Diane Trister Dodge, *The Creative Curriculum*

Chapter 5

Make time each day to... Observe

As grown-ups we put a lot of faith into that which we can see, often forgetting we have four other senses, four additional ways of taking in information. When working with children it is to our advantage, and theirs, to provide opportunities for practicing the use of *all* our senses not just that which is limited to sight, but hearing, touching, smelling and tasting too. You will find that our foundational elements of "observing" and "discussing" often go hand-in-hand. In order for children to begin observing subtleties and nuances of their environment, we must again employ the use of descriptive language as we point out what we see, smell, taste, touch, and hear while in the classroom and when outdoors.

Early on in my teaching career "My Five Senses" was a popular and frequently used weekly theme at the preschool. We liked it because there were *five* senses and *five* days of the week, how easy! We set up our lessons to explore one sense for each day. While there is nothing inherently wrong with sniffing baby food jars filled with cinnamon and cotton balls drenched in vanilla, playing "Listening Lotto" during circle time, reaching into mystery touch boxes, having tasting parties filled with exotic fruits and different blends of juices and experiencing what it's like to paint while blindfolded, over the years while learning more about teaching (and changing my mind about how I did it), I grew to realize that saving the senses for one brief week of exploration simply wasn't enough time!

I learned that when we increase our awareness of our senses we can increase the number of ways we are taking in information, thus making us able to receive more information while experiencing more of the wonder around us. There are many things in our world that we can see, look at, notice and recognize, but when was the last time you really *observed* what surrounds you? When was the last time you *listened* to the sounds coming from the neighborhood or the playground? *Felt* the textures of the pillows in the book area or the clothes in home-living? *Smelled* the scents emerging from a kitchen where applesauce is simmering and cookies are baking? *Watched* the ice block of colors melt in the afternoon sun? *Tasted* the salt on the made-from-scratch pretzels you whipped up with the children for snack?

Once again we see that not having enough *time* often becomes the roadblock to appreciating what our senses have to offer. We need to *believe* that hummingbirds sipping their sweet red nectar and mourning doves cooing in the trees are things worth paying attention to. If grown-ups feel that watching butterflies, listening to birds and feeling the grass under our barefeet are silly wastes of time, no appreciation will transpire.

There must be enough time for exploring how the ooblick feels as is drips down hands, arms and legs. There must also be an understanding that some children can spend twenty, thirty, even forty minutes exploring the texture and feel of this goopy substance of cornstarch and water. There needs to be time carved out of the day for baking, cooking and enjoying the smells that then permeate the room; along with the awareness that the *process* of smelling spices, touching ingredients and kneading dough is often more exciting and more important to children than the *product* that will emerge from the oven.

If the exploration is hurried, the experience will be lost. When we slow down enough to make and appreciate these discoveries, we unlock the door to a wider world for both ourselves, and the children. Let's take a look:

The Sense of Touch

We use our hands to take in information via our sense of touch. To experience touch, and increase the children's "touch repertoire," teachers will fill sensory tubs with such materials as: sandpaper, cooked spaghetti, pudding for painting, cornstarch, clean mud (a mixture of warm water, grated bar soap and toilet paper), cornmeal, sandbox sand, beach sand (there is a difference), birdseed, flax seed (sometimes dry, sometimes with warm water which creates a pleasing, squishy sensorial experience that calls up images of warm molasses), mud, dirt, beans, shaving cream, jello, rice, pebbles, rocks, ice, seashells, flour and sometimes, just plain old water.

We offer words such as touch, feel, sticky, wet, dry, rough, bumpy, smooth and scratchy as they describe what they feel. This is the attachment of language to their experiences. We extend activities by offering scoops, funnels and measuring cups. Forgotten and unused kitchen equipment such as muffin tins, pie tins, wooden spoons, pots and pans find new lives in the hands of little children. We offer magnifying glasses to make the birdseed bigger and safety goggles because then the children *know* they are really "working."

For children who don't want to touch with fingers and hands we offer long sticks and wooden spoons so they can still have the experience without having to actually touch. All are invited to participate at their own level of comfort. We make "touch bags" which are plastic sandwich bags filled with items like shaving cream, hair gel, corn syrup, sand or jello then sealed shut in the bag. These touch bags offer another way of experiencing new textures for children who might not yet be comfortable thrusting their whole hand in a tub of clean mud - some children like that high level of sensorial stimulation, some don't. Make room for all comfort levels and avoid forcing anyone to touch.

I also keep plastic gloves in the room – the children see us wearing them sometimes and then, of course they want to wear them. Mikey especially loves the gloves. He wears them to play in the mud, but also to ride the bike and bounce the ball. He wears them all over the school – inside! Outside! "Sa-see! Sa-see!" he cried (he never quite got "Lee-sa" as my name. To Mikey, I was "Sa-see") "Take a picture with my gloves!"

Mikey puts water in the gloves and then carries his "hand-bag" all over the place. He puts on the high heels and the feather boa and wears his gloves around the house. I know when I wear gloves things feel different, so we keep heavy duty dish gloves, mittens, winter gloves and those clear disposable gloves for the children to experience different touch and textures too. Once while I was in the kitchen washing the dishes, Mikey came into the room – I heard him before I saw him as he *always* had on the gaudy gold bridesmaid shoes from the dress up corner. He came around the corner where I was washing dishes, green heavy-duty plastic gloves up to my elbows. He actually shuttered in delight, eyes wide with longing and said, "Nice gloves Sa-see." He wore them the rest of the day.

Some children seem to really enjoy (almost crave) tactile stimulation! Have you ever worn a pair of nylons around these children? They love the texture of nylons and really enjoy rubbing, pulling and touching them. They really respond to the feel of the nylons under their little hands. Fill the environment with pillows that are made of different kinds of materials such as: satin, velour, corduroy, or anything else that provides an interesting texture.

Another fun project for touch exploration is to put a long sheet of contact paper on the floor, sticky side up! Peel off the backing, lay the contact paper down on the floor, tape it down with the sticky side up. The children really enjoy putting hands and bare feet on it! They dance on it, walk on it, tiptoe on it or sometimes just touch it with a finger or two.

You can tape bubble wrap on the floor or on a table for more tactile exploration! I keep pieces of sandpaper in the environment too. I find neat things to touch and we bring them into the space and provide them for the children, always remembering to stay sensitive to varying levels of comfort.

While enhancing our environment with *things* to touch, we must never forget the power of *human touch*. Hugging, holding hands, wrestles and romps on the lawn, sitting on laps, back rubs before naptime, quick squeezes of support and long sustained embraces of comfort all need to be a part of our daily experience with children too.

In her book, *A Natural History of the Senses,* author Diane Ackerman tells us that touch clarifies the shorthand of our eyes and reminds us that we live in a three-dimensional world.[1] Run outside and soak it up! Plunge into an icy pool of water, feel the long grass tickle your ankles, dive into that tub of ooblick, put your arms in a bowl of jello, put your bare foot in a mud puddle and feel the tension of the earth and water as you try to pull it out, feel the squish of wet sand between your toes, get a back scratch, a massage or a head rub. You are on you way to understanding the importance of touch.

The Sense of Smell

When we try to explain or describe a smell we often find ourselves at a loss for words. The sense of smell is often called the "mute sense" because it is the one with no words. We describe smells through metaphor; what they smell *like*, in terms of other things (smokey, fruity, sweet) or we describe them by how they make us feel, (intoxicating, pleasurable, disgusting, revolting).[2] The link between the language and smell center of our brain is very weak, thus our struggle with using words to describe smells.

The connection between the smell and memory centers, however, is very strong. Our sense of smell serves as our strongest link to memory. Smells become a virtual trip-wire to our memory center bringing back memories, recollections and associations triggered by that smell. What smells trigger memories for you?

Open a box of Crayola crayons and inhale deeply. What do you remember? What pictures come to your mind? How about a jar of paste? Ever walked into a crowded room and caught the scent of a former boyfriend? A past teacher? A family member?

A workshop participant recently shared that tea with lemon evokes memories of her grandmother. The smell of toasted rye bread and coffee in the percolator brings up memories of breakfast at my grandma's house. How about you?

When infants begin in our program we ask mom to sleep in the same shirt for a few days before the baby starts in the program. Then the teacher can wear the shirt draped over her own clothes so that the newborn can be connected with mom's familiar smell while making the transition to a new provider. The same idea worked for a baby once that was refusing to take a bottle. The little one just could not relax. She cried, arched her little body and seemed inconsolable. I called her mom and asked her to sleep in a t-shirt and then bring us the shirt. We draped the mom-scented shirt over our body allowing the baby to "smell" mommy while taking her bottle. Success! Eventually she no longer needed the shirt while eating, but it was a big help during that rough time.

One of my brothers has been a teacher in both Huntington Beach and Sacramento, California – one Monday morning one of his students came running into the classroom announcing, "Mr. Griffen! Mr. Griffen! I was at the mall this weekend and I *smelled* you! I looked everywhere for you but... but... but... I couldn't *find you!!*" Someone walked by during her trip to the mall wearing the same cologne as my brother! She was *sure* that her Mr. Griffen was somewhere and couldn't understand why she wasn't able to find him! After all, she could *smell* him – where did he go? Can you just see her searching the mall, "Mr. Griffen... where are you? Mr. Griffen?"

What perfume counter will *your* students walk by in five, ten, twenty years that will cause them to stop for a moment while they watch the video of memories playing in their mind's eye of the days they spent with you?

Many of the schools I visit lack "good" smells and instead only provide the smell of various cleaning fluids like Pine-Sol, Bleach and Simple Green. These are not "cozy and warm" smells. They make me think of cold, sterile hospitals and over-sanitized waiting rooms. Now don't get me wrong - you still need to *clean*. But by all means if the first thing you smell when you walk in the door every morning is bleach – *do something about it!*

Make a pot of coffee every morning even if no one drinks it! It smells good. It's warm and inviting. Make scent jars for the environment (baby food jars with spices and extracts), plant fragrant herbs and plants like rosemary, basil, heather or lavender and plunge your face in the roses. Bake bread, make pasta sauce, cookies and pies. Try putting vanilla on the light bulbs, burn candles and light incense too.

I want the children to grow up and remember me, and their time with me, when they smell chocolate chip cookies, spaghetti sauce, rosemary, patchouli oil and roses. Not when they are walking down the janitorial aisle of the grocery store, "Ah, Simple Green! Smells like Ms. Lisa's house!" No no no!!

I imagine you would want the same.

The Sense of Taste

One year, much to everyone's surprise, while boiling a purple cabbage to obtain the purple juice for a science related "acid and base" experience, four-year old MacKenzie pointed to the cabbage simmering in the skillet and announced, "I want to eat some of that!" I went to the kitchen and got her a bowl, spoon and fork and gave her some cabbage. I really didn't think she'd like it but I wasn't about to tell her she couldn't try it! MacKenzie sat down with that bowl of cabbage and ate it up so quick and with such pleasure, asking for seconds even before we realized she had started eating it, that the entire class demanded some!

Science turned into snack that day!

Cook together and eat together and take your time while eating. Chew your food and savor the flavors. We encourage our parents to pack lunches filled with food from the previous night's dinner, or a sandwich, a fruit or veggie and maybe a cookie or two. We discourage fast, easy, convenience style foods and prohibit candy and soda. No one is forced to eat and the children can eat their food in any order they like. Lunch is a time for conversation, relaxation, the discussion of the morning's events as well as the preparation for the transition to nap and rest time. It's not time for power struggles over who sits by who and other meaningless monitorings such as who ate what first.

We have family potlucks. Favorite snack day. Fruit salad parties where everyone brings their favorite fruit and we cut it all up and make a fruit salad to share. We occasionally act out the "Stone Soup" story and again share in the process of cooking, eating and sharing a meal together.

We planted an edible garden with the children so they could eat what they grew. It's amazing how the interest in beans and other veggies increases when they played a part in the creation of the food! We had cherry tomatoes, green beans, blackberries and plums available in the yard for the children to eat as they wished.

Have a "teddy bear picnic" outside or bring lunches on your next walk to the park. My mom used to say that everything tasted better when you ate it outside. I think what really happens when you eat outside is that you are removed from the visual reminders of closets that need to be cleaned, laundry that needs to be folded, around the house fix-it projects, miles of to-do lists, schedules and calendars with looming deadlines not to mention the interruptions from dinner time phone calls and the constant distraction of televisions and computers.

Removing yourself from these distractions and into the calmness and serenity of the outdoors allows you to focus your attention instead on loved ones, family, food and each delicious bite.

The Sense of Hearing

We don't often listen to each other in our culture. The typical American good morning greeting goes something like this:

"Hi! How are you?"

"OK!"

"See you later!"

"Bye!"

When asked, "How are you?" they don't really want to know – it's just what we say. You experienced this one day when they asked "How ya doin'?" and you started to actually tell them – you were kind of cranky and had a headache because the dog got out this morning and then you spilled coffee all over your new shirt in the car and then got a flat en route to school... and they still say, "OK! See ya later – Bye!"

And you are like, OHMIGOD! They weren't even listening to me!

We must practice listening – and not just listening – but *hearing*. There is a difference. It can be hard to really *hear* little children sometimes. It can take them an hour to tell you a story – and when you are trying to watch 11 other children, get Kati to the bus and change Donnell's diaper it can be easy to brush them off and say, "Not now."

Resist the urge to though. Try and stay in the moment with them and really hear them. It is hard – practice it anyway!

"Listen! What's that sound?" Is a game we play with children to heighten their classification and identification skills but also as a way for them to increase their awareness of the subtle sounds in their environment. Not just the sounds of voices, but a layer deeper, then a layer deeper, until they tell us that they hear the flowers and the wind. The best way to encourage *that* kind of awareness is to practice listening.

So we listen to and really *hear* our dog bark, the neighbor's cat purr and the many sets of wind chimes that grace the back patio. We listen to the "river" (flood channel) behind our house and the helicopters that fly over too. We listen to bees, birds and construction workers. We clink our glasses at snack time to say "cheers."

We play music of different styles for listening and dancing. We make our voices LOUD then we whisper like mice. We use instruments and bells, rattles and gourds, all when playing with sound. We talk though paper towel tubes. We purchased PVC pipe "elbows" that look like huge pieces of elbow macaroni and the children use them as phones. A workshop participant once told me that a boy in her class uses it to make "announcements." He will say things like, "Mrs. McGuinty – please report to the office, Mrs. McGuinty to the office please!"

On the back fence of our play yard we hung up washboards, pie tines, tin cans and hubcaps for the children to tap, bang and make sounds on. We took an old hose cut into 3 long pieces, a PVC T-connector and three old funnels, duct taped the whole thing together and called it "three way calling." So many things can be used to enhance the children's exploration of sound: tuning forks, large water bottles, cookie cooling trays, slinkies, hubcaps and even long sections of plastic dryer tube.

We listen to the traffic that goes by, including the city buses whose route passes in front of the schoolhouse. We run out to wave to the drivers and sometimes they stop and wave back. We stop and listen as the neighbor's Bang! Bang! Whirr! Whirr! Beep! Beep! sounds drift into our yard. The children holler out their identifications of the mystery sounds – A truck backing up! Lawnmower! Hammer! Saw! Big Truck!

And every Wednesday we anxiously anticipate the dumping crashing sounds that indicate the arrival of the trash man. Have you noticed that preschoolers absolutely adore the trash man?? He is like a *god* to them! In our community we have three trash pick ups: garbage, recycles and yard waste. This of course makes for three separate visits from every preschooler's favorite community helper. The anticipation of his arrival is almost unbearable. Eventually the sounds outside cue us that he is close, so sand toys get dropped, books are hastily put back on shelves, playdough quickly stuffed back into the bag, we all grab hands, run out front, and wait.

We watch and we wait. We wait and we watch. We listen for his brakes and his telltale horn - here he comes! We see him down the block, coming around the corner, we hear the crashing and the banging of the neighbors cans being set back down on the sidewalk, until, yes – finally – it's our turn! He jumps out and waves (all three crews know the routine now, I figure someone circulated a memo) then he dumps everything into the container on the front of the truck and always waits until we are all watching before he dumps the big container over the top and into the big barrel hidden inside the belly of the truck. Then he hops back in, waves good-bye and toots his horn as he moves on down the street.

Some children get so worked up at this juncture they can barely contain themselves, jumping up and down, arms raised high over their heads, screaming and clapping! Inside we go to anxiously await the second and third visit. Some children are so excited they are squirming and dancing, wiggling, screaming, clapping and just shaking with excitement. I don't know what it's about but they get *crazy* and all worked up!

My teachers do the same thing when the UPS man comes….

The Sense of Sight

Sense expert, Diane Ackerman, offers that abstract thinking might have evolved from the elaborate struggle of our eyes to make sense of what they saw.[3] She also points out that seventy-percent of the body's sense receptors cluster in the eyes, therefore, it is mainly through *seeing* the world that we appreciate it and understand it.

We must take measures to ensure that classrooms are visually *pleasing*, not visually *overwhelming*. Avoid cutesy, cartoony posters and instead invest in reprints of quality pieces of eye pleasing art and better yet – decorate with the children's art! I do not allow any "cute" posters in our classroom. No Barney. No Bob the Builder. No Sesame Street. And, brace yourself – no Disney. No commercialized stuff in the classroom. They get too much of that in their daily life. While children are in my care I feel it is my responsibility to shelter them from the onslaught of commercialized images that do nothing more than encourage toddlers to become shoppers. I heard once (sorry, no actual reference here) that marketing experts can actually project out a child's spending habits as a grown up *by the age if two* based on the amount of media images they receive on a daily basis. That's scary.

Be aware of the colors in the room too! Somewhere along the way we bought into the idea (myth) that school walls, fixtures and furniture need to be RED YELLOW AND BLUE. No no no! Not always true. I have walked into so many rooms that scream PRIMARY COLORS WERE USED HERE! These intense blue, yellow and red rooms are often both harsh to look at and painful to the eyes. Walk into a room with lots of red, bright yellow and dark blue and then into one with soft greens, pastel purples, and light blues...the second room will instantaneously provide a much more calming and peaceful atmosphere.

I suggest you play with pastels, neutral colors, natural shades and use wood in lieu of plastic as often as possible!

I have a friend who painted one wall of the children's playroom red. The children became louder and more aggressive within the week. After the wall was painted a more neutral color the children's behaviors went back to "normal." I have another friends who shared that her school received some donated carpet, so they put it in the nap room. However, it was *red* carpet! Within three days the children stopped napping. Red is a very energetic color and it can often bring out aggressiveness in people. It is worth the time and effort to investigate colors and their different emotional, psychological and physiological impact when decorating rooms where children (and teachers) will be spending a considerable amount of time.

Take the time and make the effort to point out and pay attention to the minor details and minuscule wonders within a child's world. I hired one of my teachers on the spot as she flopped herself down on her belly right next to the children and spent the next ten minutes silently watching ants crawl through cracks in the sidewalk. Had she flopped down and started chattering incessantly about the ants and "let's count them" and "I wonder what they are doing" I don't know if I would have been so quick to offer her a job right then and there. There is just as much talent in knowing when to talk about what you are seeing, how to use descriptive language and extend the observation with words, as there is in knowing when to just shut up.

One of my first personal hurdles as I was on my journey of becoming a professional educator, was learning how to be comfortable with silence and how to embrace stillness. I thought I always had to say something or make a comment. It took a long time before I gave myself permission to simply look, not feeling the need to look look look and then make a comment. If we aren't cautious, words can take away from the sensation. Educator Alfie Kohn said, "Terrific teachers have teeth marks on their tongues."[4] There is power in quiet.

Notice and discuss what happens to rain puddles after the sun comes out from behind the clouds. Follow the cricket that just hopped into the room. Watch the birds eating at the feeders outside. Look at the ants on the floor. Begin observing differences and subtle nuances within your environment. Observe out loud what, *to you*, might seem obvious - someone might have missed something.

As children get older you can begin to observe more detailed things like the differences between hardboiled eggs and raw eggs, ice and water or primary colors mixing to make secondary colors. Point out opposites and give children concrete examples to attach to observations of hot and cold, wet and dry, fast and slow.

Observe and discuss what happens to eggs in salt water and eggs in tap water. What happens when you put rock salt on ice? When you mix flour and water? When you pour vinegar into a pie tin filled with baking soda? When a pinecone falls into a tub of water? What happens? What do you see?

Time, patience and awareness is what broadens the superficial exploration of a few textured carpet squares and baby food jars filled with stale, leftover spices during My Five Senses Week, to a life-long understanding and appreciation of the sights, smells, textures, tastes and sounds available to us when we see the value in pausing to observe them.

The Importance of Observing... In Review:

1. Making more time to observe means increasing the number of opportunities we provide for children to be engaged with *all* their senses instead of only focusing on one or two.

2. Make sure "observing" isn't reduced to a checklist of the five senses! Smell this – check! Touch this – check!

3. Time must be set aside to show the importance of noticing (smelling, hearing, ect) what is happening in the world around us.

4. Reducing observing to "Five Senses Week" might be rather limiting – instead think of what can be done each day to facilitate the development of awareness.

Some things to think about

1. Are we making enough time for deeper levels of awareness and observation?

2. Am I stuck in the "My Five Senses" approach?

3. What can we do to increase opportunity for Tasting? Listening? Touching? Smelling? Seeing?

4. How am I working on embracing the power of silence?

5. What do I smell immediately upon entering my school?

6. My classroom?

7. The playroom?

8. How can I (or have I) make/made it more pleasant?

9. How might I make my environment more visually pleasing?

10. What decorates our walls?

11. Might this need to be modified?

12. Do we have enough time in the day to make a point of noticing (hearing, seeing, experiencing) the things around us?

13. What is one thing I can do Monday to begin making more time each day for observing?

Notable and Quotable

Perfume is liquid memory.

-Diane Ackerman, *A Natural History of the Senses*

If you want to do something good for a child…give him an environment where he can touch things as much as he wants.

-Buckminster Fuller in *Letter to Children on Earth*
Seen on a plaque posted outside of a preschool in Los Angeles.

All knowledge begins in observation.

-Robert and Michelle Root-Bernstein, *Sparks of Genius*

How ya doin?
OK
See ya later
Bye

-Typical American morning greeting

If your knack for observation is not skillful enough to permit you to sketch a man falling out a window during the time it takes him to fall from the 5th story to the ground, you will never produce monumental work.

-Eugene Delacroix, Henri Matisse's art teacher

Chapter 6

Make time each day to...Read

"Look look look! *Ann Likes Red!* I remember this one, oh and *Mog the Forgetful Cat!* This one was my *favorite! Here's Eighteen Cousins* and even *Miss Suzy*! And look - *Mike Mulligan!*" You'd have thought that the five of us were preschool children on our first field trip to the library, not teenagers and twenty somethings helping mom and dad "pack" for their move to their new house. Although we all had been summoned to the house to help mom and dad move, my brothers, sister and I spent more time rummaging *through* boxes than actually packing and moving them.

We fell into the couch and chairs in the living room with our piles of childhood storybooks surrounding us on the floor and heaped in our laps. We flipped through pages, recited favorite passages and shared the pictures with each other as though seeing them for the first time. We shared the memories that surrounded the books for us; where we remembered reading them and who the book was a present from. We recalled certain passages that made us feel scared or happy and found torn pages that had been ripped out in a fit of childhood anger (the cause of which was long forgotten) and we rediscovered just how much, as children, we identified with the characters, even going so far as to think we *were* the characters in some of the stories.

Heavy sighs coming from our tired, hard-working parents, along with glances over glasses and gazes from around corners were giving us nonverbal cues to leave the books alone, put them back in the box, and get back to the task at hand!

We kept reading!

When mom came in to finally shoo us off couches and out of chairs we pleaded with her to be able to take our favorites with us to our own houses, but to no avail! The books of our past were going to the new house where they would be ready and waiting for the, at that time, nonexistent grandchildren. We whined and complained so much you'd have thought we were stubborn children in the midst of a tantrum! We resumed our packing, but not before hiding a few favorites in purses and backpacks! We weren't going to leave those memories and that history behind.

In her book, *Inside Picture Books*, author Ellen Handler Spitz tells us, "We never seem to forget our first books: the look, feel, smell of pages daubed with color that pulled us in when we were small. Just a name - Madeline, Corduroy, Ferdinand, Max and his wild things – brings an image, or the fragments of a story, the timbre of someone's reading voice, the folds of the quilt and the sensation of being held by someone, being together, while enveloped in fantasy." [1]

In order for children to have these memories, create connections with characters, get lost in the fantasy and remember the folds of the quilt while being held, we need to make time for those memories to be made. Simply having a book center in the classroom is not promoting a love of reading; especially when, as was the case of a school I once visited, the book center contained nothing but copies of *Glamour* magazine.

In addition to creating a book center, with cozy pillows, filled with high-quality picture books, we must read to them. Bev Bos says we must, "Read! Read! Read! Until you think your lips are going to fall off – and then - read one more!" And we must read "good" books. Children do not stumble onto good books by themselves; they must be introduced to them. [2] And just what makes a "good book?" In her book, *Dear Mem Fox, I have Read All your Books Even the Pathetic Ones*, acclaimed children's author, Mem Fox says: "good books have as much to do with the effect they have on the reader as with any other criterion. If we don't laugh, gasp, howl, block our ears, sigh, vomit, giggle, curl our toes, empathize, sympathize, feel pain, weep or shiver during the reading of a picture book, then surely the writer has wasted our time, our money and our precious, precious trees." [3]

I have included a list of some of my favorite books and authors at the end of this chapter for you.

As teachers who barely make enough money to live on, it can be tempting to purchase the bucket o'books we find at a garage sale, cheap, yet often of poor quality, ripped and torn. We might wonder if it's worth the money spent on hardback books if "all the children do is rip them." Yet what kind of messages are we sending if our book centers are filled with books that are ripped and have torn pages?   How can we expect them to not rip them if those are the only kinds of books we are offering them? If we *expect* that the children will rip books, they will. If, however, we teach them how to handle books, treat them with care, put them away when finished and point out rips, tears and pages in need of repair so helpful grown-up hands can fix them. We are teaching skills that will not only encourage the love of books, but the respect of them as well.

I once worked as a substitute in a classroom where the last few pages of a certain book were missing; someone had torn them out and the book was never mended or replaced. I brought in my own copy of this particular book so the children could see the missing pictures and hear how the story ended - but they wanted nothing to do with it! When we read through my copy, eventually getting to the page where theirs had been torn, they wanted to go no further and insisted that *that* was the end of the book!

Make the investment and purchase good books. Two or three hardback favorites are better than a box filled with hundreds of ripped and torn commercialized books. Also, buy a big thick roll of clear packing tape so that when the books get ripped and torn (which they will) the children can assist you as you fix them. There is no better way to model the value and importance of books.

Once while out on a sub job the teacher's "sub note" for me indicated that the "good books" were to be kept in the teacher cupboard and were for "teacher hands only." Children were allowed to only look at the books in the book center. Upon looking at the books in the center I was disgusted. Ripped, torn, old stories, horrible pictures, arugh!

Put the "good books" out. Then take responsibility for showing them how to use them!

Babies need chubby board books with pictures of real objects in them, along with books that encourage their involvement, like *Pat the Bunny*. Be sure baby's book basket also includes board book re-prints of classics such as *Good Night Moon* and *Brown Bear Brown Bear*. Even though they are not yet verbal and might not *appear* interested (yet), reading to baby now sets the stage for an enjoyment of stories as they grow up and begins the ritual of appreciating, listening, looking and cuddling up with a book. Plus it allows the adults to get into the routine and habit of reading to children whenever possible, as often as possible for as long as possible.[4]

For preschoolers, provide engaging books that promote questions and discussions. Read aloud to children often and allow them to read to each other too. Remember what we learned about children needing to talk out loud to process their thoughts? A group of preschoolers reading out loud on the carpet both to themselves and each other disturbs no one except the teacher who is demanding a quiet classroom.

Provide books with lush, detailed pictures and a meaningful story line, not something designed to be preachy or teachy. You want to find stories that promote questions and discussions immediately on page one. Older toddlers and preschoolers will begin to sit for longer story times; be sure to have paper back and hardbound editions of classics, and multiple copies of classroom favorites. If the children don't get involved, don't ask questions and don't seem interested in the book being read, by all means put it down and pick a different one. There is no hard and fast rule that says you must finish a book just because you started it! *Our goal is **not** "to get to the end of the book!"*

The purpose of reading is not solely just to finish the book, but also to enjoy great stories by great authors. I have been known to start a story for children, only to still be on page one after fifteen minutes because everyone had something to say about the picture or the story! Set aside the self-induced pressure of "needing to finish the book." If you are simply reading in order to hurry up, turn the page, and finish the book, you miss out on sharing an amazing experience with the children.

If you are tired or angry – in a bad mood or simply otherwise grouchy – don't take it out on the book! Ask the child to read to you, take a minute to calm down. Then read a book to them. Tape record yourself reading your child's favorite book. Five times in a row. Then have a friend read the book. Five times in a row. Then dad and grandma too. This tape will be a lifesaver for when you are extra tired and don't want to read, for when you are absent or when your child just wants something different.

We are blessed to have made an audiotape of my grandma reading all our favorite books to us before she died. My sister's favorite is grandma's rendition of *The Jolly Postman*. Grandma even changed up her voice for all the letters the postman delivered. Treasures such as these are priceless. Make some for your family and classroom.

Always read a book on your own before reading it to a group of children. From this, you can use Mem Fox's criteria to see if it is a "good book," develop a feeling for the characters and the story line and determine whether or not it is appropriate for your age group.

A quality book corner will include easy books, just right books and books that are a wee bit challenging. This way, when they are ready for something a little more complex, it is already on-hand for their enjoyment. I also read stories to the children that do not have any pictures. I do this so that children can practice making their own pictures in their heads! I tell stories from the top of my head and also do visualizations with the children. I tell the children, "I'm going to tell you a story – see if you can make the pictures appear in your head!" I see this as good practice for children who are growing up in a media drenched culture where all of their images are being created for them!

Books are read inside, outside, in trees and under them. Books are read on swings and before naptime and there are books available in the bathrooms. Books are brought on neighborhood walks to the park and on picnics too. Books are not mandated to stay in the book area. Family related stories are in the dress up center and home living. Building, construction and transportation books are added to the block corner. Time is made for one-on-one reading with children as well as planned group story times too.

Don't save reading only for group time or circle time! Reading should be happening all day long!

Feel free to alter the names in the story by substituting the name(s) of someone in the class for characters in the story and give yourself permission to play with the words in the story too. I once spent an entire circle time with a group of four year olds doing nothing but substituting words in the title of *The Little Mouse, The Red Ripe Strawberry and The Big Hungry Bear*. The children were roaring with laughter, rolling on the carpet and doubled over with glee. They were hollering out their own suggestions too and after some time we all decided that our favorite was *The Little Boy, The Red Ripe Banana and The Big Hungry Bellybutton!* Hushing and shushing their joyful outbursts in order to "read the book" would have squashed the use of descriptive language, destroyed the laughter and the killed the experience completely. We eventually got around to reading the book all the way through and it quickly became a popular favorite. Each time we would pull it off the shelf for group time the children would say, "Remember the day we made up all those words?!"

I encourage you to avoid commercialized books that reinforce television viewing and turn preschoolers into consumers. By this I mean avoiding books that are nothing more than commercials for TV shows, cartoons and the preschool icons d'jour such as Barney, the Sesame Street characters, Pokemon, Power Rangers, Power Puff Girls, Barbie, Teletubbies, Bob the Builder or Disney.

Never under any circumstances tell a child who might be in trouble to, "Go sit down and read a book," or to "Go sit in the book corner." True, the book corner might be a quiet area that is conducive to calming down, but in reality you are *linking being in trouble with reading.* Not a very positive association. In addition, a child who is worked up and out of control is in no condition to sit independently and read a book. (And we wonder why the pages get ripped...) Can *you* concentrate on reading when you are mad, angry or upset? Of course not! A better suggestion might be to go *with* this child to the rocking chair, and, while holding him on your lap spend some time together.

In addition, classrooms that still use writing as punishment really need to begin questioning this practice too. Demanding children to write a sentence 100 times or to write on the board what they will not do anymore does nothing but kill their desire to write *anything.* There is a discipline handbook that advises non-compliant school-aged children be "asked to perform an unpleasant task such as a simple writing assignment."[5] All this does is discourage any potential interest in the arena of writing. Be careful not to fall into the traps that use reading and writing as punishment.

If you really want your children to be excited about reading then make sure they see you reading too! Children in some homes never see their parents concentrate on anything for a considerable amount of time except the television![6] Television, computers, video games, fax machines, beepers, cell phones and busy schedules become the enemies of reading and keep us away from books, stories and family reading nights. Remember that we teach children what is valuable by the way they see us spending our own time. Turn off the TV, shut off the computer, stop answering the phone and permit your children to see you engrossed in a book! There is a story about a five- year old girl who snatched a book from her father and, eyes fixed with frustration and determination, passionately demanded, "Tell me what it is! Tell me what it says! Read it to me!" [7] She was certain it must be fascinating because he had not taken his eyes off it for an hour!

By linking stories to experiences we can make even a bigger impact. For example, when reading *Blueberries for Sal,* have **real** blueberries available to eat. The house across the street from our schoolhouse went through a complete remodeling. There were bulldozers and dump trucks in front of the house for weeks! We linked this experience up with many books that expanded on what the children were actually witnessing in the front yard! When Ian came back to school from his camping trip announcing he had seen a bear (they really had) we found a resurgence of interest in all our bear oriented books! Books and experience go together.[8]

It is also to our advantage if we learn the art of how to read a story to children. I have had countless teachers tell me that they don't understand why the children in their class refuse to come to story time. Then I listen to these teachers read a story. Flat, garbled, soft-spoken, boring, monotone recounts of *Where The Wild Things Are* does not capture the emotion of the story! Quick paced, hurry-up-and-get-to-the-end readings of *The Napping House* or *The Very Hungry Caterpillar* that are broken up only by the teacher's frazzled and annoyed commands of "Sit still!" "Get on your bottom!" "Criss-cross applesauce!" "1-2-3! Eyes on me!" and "SHHHHHH!! I'm reading!" ruin the flavor of the story and the overall purpose of gathering to read the story in the first place – to come together to experience a good book.

I suggest at some point in their career, teachers make a tape of themselves reading to children. Then listen to it. How is the sound? Pitch? Is there intonation, a moving up and down pattern, to their speech? Do they use volume for emphasis, calling on both loud and quiet to add flavor to the story? Or is it monotone? Do they read too fast? Too slow? When we become better at reading, the children become better at listening.

One of the hardest jobs I have had is attempting to convince parents and teachers that when it comes to strengthening the foundation of reading, all they really need is twenty minutes of reading time and a library card. Even if you can afford to purchase a collection of books for your home, you and your child will still benefit from having a library card. Visit the library at your child's school, support your local community library, attend story time, get to know the librarians and demand the continued purchase of books. Many school libraries are being turned into computer labs, book-purchasing budgets are cut in order to purchase technological equipment and librarians are being replaced with "information specialists." If we aren't careful our libraries will turn into sterile information warehouses filled with computer workstations and devoid of caring individuals.[9]

The library is a valuable community resource and I encourage you to visit it with the children as often as possible. The library houses so much more than books. It holds information, keys to history, past and present knowledge, passports to adventures and most of all, people. Not only people who know just what we're looking for and who can suggest something when we don't, people who assist us with research reports and help us master the new catalog, but other people too, community members, neighbors, lonely people, happy people, children, grandpas and families, who, as different as they might look and be, share in the love of reading and believe in the power of books.

FAVORITE BOOKS FOR CHILDREN

Abiyoyo, Pete Seeger

Alexander and the Terrible Horrible No Good Very Bad Day, Judith Viorst

Animals Should Definitely NOT Wear Clothing, Judi Barrett

Blueberries for Sal, Robert McCloskey

Borreguita and the Coyote, Verna Aardema

Brown Bear Brown Bear, Eric Carle

Caps for Sale, Esphyr Slobodinka

Catch the Baby, Lee Kingman

Chicka Chicka Boom Boom, Bill Martin Jr.

Cinder Eyed Cats, Eric Rohmann

Cloudland, John Burningham

Corduroy, Don Freeman

Darkness, Mildred Pitts Walter

Don't Fidget a Feather, Erica Silverman

Dooly and the Snortlesnoot, Jack Kent

Emma's Eggs, Margaret Ruurs

Giant Jam Sandwich, The, John Vernon Lord

Good Dog Carl, Alexandra Day

Good Night Gorilla, Peggy Rathman

Gotcha!, Gail Jorgensen

Happy Birth Day, Robie Harris

How The Sun Was Brought Back to the Sky, Mirra Ginsburg

I Love You the Purplest, Barbara Joosse

If, Sarah Perry

Imogene's Antlers, David Small

Ira Sleeps Over, Bernard Waber

It Looked Like Spilt Milk, Charles Shaw

It's The Bear!, Jez Alborough

Leo the Late Bloomer, Robert Kraus

Little Blue and Little Yellow, Leo Lionni

Little House, The, Virginia Lee Burton

Little Mouse, Red Ripe Strawberry and Big Hungry Bear, The, Don & Audrey Wood

Little Old Lady Who Was Not Afraid of Anything, The, Linda Williams

Madeline, Ludwig Bemelmans

Magic Quilt, The, Blair Thompson

Mama Zooms, Jane Cowen-Fletcher

Monster Mama, Liz Rosenberg

More More More Said the Baby!, Vera Williams

Mortimer, Robert Munsch

Murmel Murmel Murmel, Robert Munsch

My Daddy, Susan Paradis

My Dog Rosie, Isabelle Harper

Night Driving, John Coy

No, David!, David Shannon

Our Granny, Margaret Wild

Owl Babies, Martin Waddell

Owl Moon, Jane Yolen

Purple Green and Yellow, Robert Munsch

Quick as a Cricket, Audrey Wood

Relative's Came, The, Cynthia Rylant

Snowy Day, The, Ezra Jack Keats

Somebody and the Three Bears, Marilyn Tolhurst

Sophie, Mem Fox

Special Kind of Love, A, Stephen Michael King

Stephanie's Ponytail, Robert Munsch

Thomas' Snowsuit, Robert Munsch

Tikki Tikki Tembo, Arlene Mosel

Time Flies, Eric Rohmann

Tough Boris, Mem Fox

Tuesday, David Wiesner

Very Hungry Caterpillar, The, Eric Carle

Where the Wild Things Are, Maurice Sendak

The Importance of Reading... In Review:

1. Children who grow up to be readers are children who have been read to.

2. Our goal is not to "get to the end of the book" but rather to instill of love of reading and of stories.

3. Change up the character names and even the title to be more playful or expressive.

4. It is OK for children to interrupt the story with questions and comments.

5. It is not required to buy lots of books – instead, use the library!

6. Books that were read to you as a child are powerful bridges between you, your past and your children.

Some things to think about

1. Are we making enough time for reading stories?

2. Do we have "good books" available?

3. How much reading am I doing on my own time?

4. Am I ready yet to tape record myself while reading to children?

5. Do I have someone I could process the outcome with?

6. What books do I remember from my childhood?

7. Who read to me when I was little?

8. Were books a priority in my home growing up?

9. How has that influenced the role of books and reading in my classroom?

10. What is one thing I can do Monday to begin making more time each day to read?

Notable and Quotable

"No book is really worth reading at the age of 10 when not equally worth reading at the age of 50."

-C.S. Lewis

The best time to start reading aloud to a baby is the day it is born.

-Mem Fox

If you want your children to be smart, read them fairy tales.
If you want them to be real smart, read them more fairy tales.

-Albert Einstein

"Read, read, read, read, and, when you think your lips are going to fall off, read one more!"

-Bev Bos

The single most important activity for building skills essential for reading success appears to be reading aloud to children. [10]

-Susan B Neuman, Assistant Secretary of Education

Chapter 7

Make time each day to... Play

When I do workshops about the importance of early experiences I tell the audience that "Play" is not a separate seventh thing within the foundation but is rather the cement that is keeping the entire thing together. I have said this a few times throughout the book and will say it again - *Play is the cement that keeps our foundation together.* When our foundation is strong, the house of higher learning – the house of "academics" can be built. And the house will be strong because the foundation supporting it is strong as well. And the foundation supporting it all consists of play.

Everything we have talked about up until now has been grounded in play – creating is playing, moving is playing, singing is playing, discussing is playing, observing is playing and reading is playing. Learning is playing and playing is learning.

It is important to point out that adults and children have different definitions of play. Play, to an adult, might be to engage in a fun activity that has a tangible result or end product such as sewing a dress, making a quilt, planting a garden, refinishing the boat, playing a softball game, running a marathon or building a shed.

The way a child wants to play is often very different from what parents or teachers might think is best. To some adults, child play appears disconnected, having no readily observable focus or goals, and no real end product. It takes time to learn how to see below the surface and witness the unlocking of the door of learning that is contained within play.

Child play is filled with loose parts, bits and pieces, sticks, balls, rocks, snails, dolls, mud, water, bikes and skateboards. There is quite a bit of milling around. Much emphasis on the gathering of things and, oftentimes, long periods of time talking about the "rules" of the game. And while the grown-ups are standing around, anxiously waiting for the play to start, they do not see that it has already begun.

The planning of the play and the setting of the stage is a vital part of the play. Deciding who gets the blue horse, who will be the baby kitty, who will push the red truck and who will get the green shovel are all essential pieces of the playing puzzle. Some argue that this discussion and deciding is more important than actually playing. This is very frustrating for the antsy grown-up onlookers who are anxious for the roads to be built, the block tower created and the tea party to start. We have forgotten that play has a process, not just a final outcome.

Most grown-ups have childhood amnesia[1] and because of this we have forgotten what it is like to be little! Therefore, we inadvertently redirect, shut off and stifle what is really developmentally appropriate child play because we think that we are being well meaning grown-ups who are teaching our children to stop running about wasting time. We must pause to remember that *childhood play is a very intellectual activity overflowing with opportunities for problem solving and creativity*. In order to really begin believing and understanding this though, we must first allow ourselves to remember what it was like when we were children.

How did you play when you were little? Where did you play? What did you do? Who was with you? How did you spend those lazy summer days? What did you do each day after school? Where were the grown-ups? How old were the other children you played with? How did you know when it was time to come home? What did you do on Saturdays? On Sundays?

I call this process getting back to the "pre" – stopping for a minute and thinking about what was it like before we grew up and decided we had the answers to everything. Until we allow ourselves to begin the process of remembering we will continue to tell children to, "Stop!" or "Come over here and do something else!" and we will continue to be so very concerned and worried that they aren't *doing* anything when in fact they are *doing* a lot, we have just forgotten what it is.

What was it like to see a bubble for the first time? Can you remember when you finally reached the pedals on your new bicycle? Did you ever eat paste? What was your feeling when you made it across the monkey bars for the first time? Do you recall the feel of squishing playdough the first time? How about making a mud pie? Do you remember squeezing glue on your hands and waiting for it to dry so you could peel it off?

By allowing ourselves to remember things like this we become better teachers, parents and educators because we are on the road of remembering the power of play and the importance of making time for it.

It is said that, "You do not stop playing when you get old – you get old because you stop playing." We must start playing again! Not only for ourselves but also for our children. We must remember the importance of play otherwise our children will miss out on so much! With long hours spent in childcare, piano lessons, gymnastics, soccer and dance class, not to mention the constant distraction of television and computers, we might find ourselves asking, "Where has all the play time gone?" One mother, in response to learning her child's friend was "all booked up" and didn't have time for a play date remarked, "it seems that children are always on their way to somewhere."[2]

Just because WE are overworked, tired, overscheduled and stressed, doesn't mean we must pass these characteristics on to our children. On one of my travels I met a woman who had a day-planner for her four year-old in order to keep track of her childs extracurricular activities. Formal scheduled play-dates with friends were wedged in-between violin lessons, dance class, birthday parties, soccer games, computer classes, and (I could only assume) her shrink.

Time is necessary for meaningful play. When children are shuffled from one activity to the next simply because that is what the schedule says it's time to do, no one is receiving the full benefit of the experience. Many preschools chop up the day into manageable twenty minute time blocks. Twenty minutes is not enough time for anything! It takes some children a good ten minutes just to choose what activity they want to do when they come to school each morning! So they spend ten minutes choosing, five minutes playing and another five minutes being told that it's now time to clean up! "Clean up?" they say, "clean up? I haven't even *done* anything yet!!"

And after awhile, if this pattern is allowed to continue, guess what happens? *They stop playing.* One group of children I was subbing with told me, "Miss Lisa, we used to build big block towers, but it was always time to put them away." The children realized there was never enough time anyway, so why bother.

Why bother indeed. If it is always time to put it away, why even bother taking it off the shelf? If there is no time to paint, why even bother purchasing an easel? If there is no time to go outside, why bother having bikes? If there is no time for singing why bother making instruments? If there is no time for talking, why bother even coming together as a group? If there is not time for observing, why bother noticing anything? If there is no time for reading, why bother writing new stories? If there is no time for playing...

You get the idea.

If there is no time for playing, our house of higher learning is going to crumble to the ground. Playing is the cement that holds our foundation of creating, moving, singing, discussing, observing and reading together and cement needs time to dry so the foundation can be solid and sturdy. The foundation needs to be strong because it is going to support the house of higher learning. The cycle needs both components in order to be complete. *We must stop demanding houses where there are no foundations!*

When children are playing with blocks they are learning about *balance* as they stack them, about *shapes* as they figure out the ones they need for their tower, about *estimating* as they figure out how many more blocks are needed for their house. They *measure* as they determine the length of the road for their cars and they learn about *gravity* when it all comes crashing down. They learn *persistence* when they pick up the pieces to start all over again and *patience* when it doesn't turn out right the first time. They explore *math* concepts as they fit six small squares together to make one big rectangle and begin to experiment with *elements of design* when adding other available "things," such as pieces of fabric, thread spools, milk caps and corks to their wooden towers.

When dressing up and playing in the house corner they are learning about manners, social roles and valuable communication skills. They are expanding their creativity while pretending and enhancing their imaginations.

When painting they are working through the stages of scribbling, experimenting with color and design, mixing primary colors to make secondary ones, learning about shape placement and engaging in self expression.

When doing puzzles they are solving problems, learning to concentrate, figuring out how things fit together and learning to see a whole from its parts.

When splashing in water they are learning about evaporation, absorption, as well as mastering the small motor skills necessary for pouring without spilling.

When doing basic science experiments they are learning about cause and effect, properties of water, density, how to make comparisons, understanding opposites as well as being able to experience messy, ooey gooey materials in an environment suitable for exploration.

When in the sand box they are measuring, scooping, discovering saturation points, learning about irrigation when draining puddles after a rain storm, learning how to cooperate as well having time for problem solving and sharing practice.

When running around, chasing each other, climbing trees and rocks they are strengthening their bodies and mastering the large motor skills which will in turn support the small motor skill development which is necessary for eventually holding pencils and crayons.

When singing and exploring musical instruments children are learning about sounds. They are exploring rhythm and patterns - all which will assist them later on as they begin to study math. In addition, music connects children to their families and communities on a social level through the continuation of songs and other cultural traditions.

When discussing and observing, children are using their senses to unlock the beauty of the world and acquiring the necessary skills to speak with others about what they are experiencing. Children realize they can learn from others in order to broaden their own horizons and that conversation is a give and take process. Discussing plants the seeds of problem solving and teaches children that they have the power to deal with conflict with their words, not their fists. Developing and nurturing social and emotional skills is truly how we work to "get children ready for school."

When reading, children are learning the importance of books. They are cultivating an understanding of their language. They are being exposed to words, thoughts and ideas that will link back to their own lives, thus strengthening the connection between experience and books. We know that if we really want to raise a generation of readers, children must be read to and they must see us reading as well.

It is quite evident that play is not simply mindless, meaningless, self-amusement. Yet, as educators, we are often required to defend the value and importance of play in the lives of children. At what point will we no longer have to constantly justify play by attaching the actions we see in play to cognitive concepts or rationalized skills that somehow make play more acceptable to the watchful, often judgmental eyes of parents, center directors, teachers, superintendents and most grown-ups in general?

If We Call it Science, Then Can We Let them Play?[3]

Sometimes we get so caught up in the whirlwind of needing to know what children are *doing* when they are playing that we forget the fact that sometimes it is okay to play simply for the sheer fun of it. It has been stated that the very existence of research about play indicates that we are a very serious society capable of taking the fun out of almost anything, including fun itself.[4] Wallowing around in the mire and muck of childhood wonders, sometimes referred to as "galumphing," needs to be permitted in our homes and in our schools.[5]

Play is important even when it does not look like anything! All play is essential to the complete development of our children, not just the play that can be linked back to a "science word." What do I mean by this? I mean that creating ooblick, the mixture of cornstarch and water, simply for the sake of making ooblick is a valuable experience worthy of exploration!! The fact that it is also introducing concepts such as action/reaction, cause/effect, evaporation, absorption and giving a very basic knowledge of the creation of Non-Newtonian fluids (a substance that has the properties of a solid and a liquid at the same time) are all bonus points! Extra credit! Ooblick is an amazing sensorial experience that activates socialization as children talk about how it feels when it drips down their arms, problem solving, measuring and estimation as they figure out just how much water makes the "perfect batch," and small motor development as they squeeze and squish it with their hands and fingers. To only do ooblick because it provides exposure to chemistry and that is a curriculum requirement two times a week limits the experience for all who are involved. Teachers are then only doing it to meet a requirement and children are only provided the allotted time to experience it. Why bother?

Yes, professional educators, family childcare providers and preschool teachers need to be able to articulate the learning that is happening when these experiences are provided *but not at the expense of taking the playfulness and fun out of the experience.* Professional educators need to have a working knowledge of the research and literature that supports a play based teaching philosophy, and, when asked, they need to be able to articulate what they know and apply it to the experiences being offered to the children in their programs. Linking it back, yes. Needing to prove it, no.

The *proving* of the importance of play has already been done. We have years of research that documents the many benefits of play as fostering and encouraging the intellectual, social, emotional, physical, language and spiritual development of our children. In light of this existing research it would seem, then, that our job would be to apply this knowledge in schools and classrooms. Or so it would appear. For many educators this is just simply not the case. Many educators find themselves in environments where, for whatever reason, it is still necessary for them to *prove* that play is very important.

We should no longer have to defend the value of play in the lives of children!

Yet by still being required and expected to justify every action that looks like "play" and not like "learning" we become distracted from our real job of creating engaging environments that meet the developmental needs of children. We spend hours arming ourselves with an arsenal of information so we are ready at a moments notice for our ongoing battle with the naysayers. We find ourselves constantly on-guard, prepared and ready at all times to defend ourselves and prove our point. It can be tiring. It makes us frustrated. It's also rather demeaning.

How annoying it becomes when, as professionals, we earn degrees, participate in extra classes, read journals, have thick studies of child development by our bedside, go to conferences, spend our own money to enhance the environments we create for the children, learn new skills, talk shop at dinner parties (much to the dismay of our significant others), share ideas with colleagues and make efforts to constantly expand our horizons and our understanding of what we do only to be treated as though we don't know what we are talking about.

At what point will the job we do be valued enough and considered professional enough that when we share our words, statements, discoveries and insights, they are believed?! Not shrugged off, not discounted, and thought to be just "fluff," (as one parent told me once). When people go to the doctor they don't demand to see the latest article that supports the diagnosis or the lab report analyzing the new antibiotic which was prescribed. Yet *our* practices are constantly questioned, demanding us to be armed with an arsenal of information, ready at a moments notice to defend the importance of play. Why isn't it accepted that we, as teachers and educators, like doctors, business folk and scientists, know what we are talking about too?

I had a thought as to *why not* during the writing of this book. I began realizing that the people we run into on a daily basis are professionals and experts in their field, whether it be law, medicine, government, business, architecture, interior design, customer service, retail, whatever – they know about their field and make every effort to stay abreast of their area of expertise. When we have questions and need answers about a topic in their profession, we call upon someone like them to assist us because they know things about their field that we don't – they are the experts.

At the same time, we too have chosen to become experts. However our area of expertise is children. *Their children.* Children *are* our profession and by having elected that path we have made it our job to know about children, schools, education, activities, stages, developmental issues and all the stuff that comes along with a major in early childhood education or child development. Appearing professional and knowing our stuff can mistakenly be interpreted as telling other people how to raise their children. Follow me on this? When contractors know their stuff they do their job, build a great fence, you love your new fence and everyone is happy. When chefs know their stuff, do their job, buy the right ingredients and prepare a delicious dish, you love your dinner and everyone is happy. When we, as educators know our stuff and do our job we're sometimes told, "Don't tell me how to raise my child."

Ouch.

A Dream?

My dream is that someday when we say the children "played today," not only will it bring up images of squished orange piles of playdough pancakes, loopy scribbled circles, story times and blue and yellow water squirted in the air with turkey basters, but it will automatically be understood to mean lessons in math, language and science. It will mean that the children were actively involved in creating ideas and exploring environments. I fantasize that the grown-ups will immediately recognize that this means problem solving and the development of shared understandings all of which were being facilitated by caring professional adults who are *experts* in their field, who know what they are talking about and know what they are doing.

I was recently fortunate enough to hear a lecture by Dr. Thomas Armstrong who, regarding play in the lives of children, made a very interesting comment. He expressed concern that without play, our culture will stop evolving and thus perish. Here is what he had on his overhead:

Experiences + Imagination = Something New[6]

According to Armstrong, the "something new" is what continues to move a culture forward. *In order to cultivate imagination we need playful, creative thinkers who have been provided time to cultivate these characteristics.*

A teacher I had used to say, "everything new is half familiar." Good programs are programs that build on this idea. They realize children need consistency and that they thrive on repetition while at the same time benefiting from exposure to rich, meaningful, engaging experiences. Good programs provide children with enough time to wallow in experiences, figure things out and think things through. Good programs hire teachers to serve as facilitators and extenders of the play. They employ adults who deserve to be treated like a professional because they act like one, not just because they have enough units.

What is a "Good" Program?

Please be aware of the fact that you cannot identify good programs by their names, locations or affiliations with certain philosophies. The distinction between "nursery school," "preschool," "childcare center" and "daycare" is nothing more than superficial verbiage.

I have seen bad schools in upper class neighborhoods and excellent schools in poor ones. I have seen authentic, high-quality Montessori schools and I have also observed places that claimed affiliation because they "bought the stuff." I have seen family childcare homes where children are cared for by loving professional providers and ones where car seats filled with babies line the hallway. I have called high dollar private schools on the phone to inquire about their philosophy and be told one thing – only to call back a few days later and be told something completely different.

I have met excellent, professional teachers who would lay their lives down for their children and I have also met the ones who yell at children when they think no one is watching. I want you to know that both kinds of these teachers are in preschools, family childcare homes, elementary schools, public schools, private schools, half-day schools and full day schools.

We must pull our heads out of the sand and take our power back. It is our job to make sure the places where children are spending their days are in their utmost, highest and best interest.

Zip codes, glossy brochures and Internet cameras do not guarantee quality. Teachers must take responsibility to ensure their classroom is the best it can be. Administrators must do the same for the school. And I'm talking about best it can be *for the children* – not simply focusing on what makes it easier for us, the adult! Owners need to find the balance between the neat and tidy "bottom line" and the not always so neat and tidy job of providing for children and their families. Parents must take responsibility in choosing quality places. Ask questions! Show up at all hours! Beware of any place that makes you call first. Take responsibility for your choice. Do not put your child in the first place you tour simply because YOU need childcare by tomorrow! It might be easier for you – but what about the child?

There is no guarantee that one "kind" of program is "better" than another simply because of what the program calls itself or because of where it is located. The proof is in the pudding. Does the program provide experiences that are grounded in a play based, developmentally appropriate philosophy? Or are they doing worksheets, dittos and academic drills in the name of "getting ready for kindergarten?"

Choosing a program just because all your friends go there when *you do not like what you see there* is not a healthy decision for you or for your child! You must look around, take tours, look beyond the brochure and really *see* what is happening in the environment.

You will be able to identify a good one when you see it. More often than not you will be able to identify one when you walk in the door. It is noisy, there are teachers on the floor, not standing around, there is child-centered art on the bulletin boards, not twenty identical cows made out of paper plates that the teacher glued together, there are tables with engaging activities on them, there are children inside and outside, there are no "time out" chairs and there are no computers. You will hear laughter and singing and you will see smiling faces. You will see teachers modeling problem solving techniques and redirecting when necessary. There will be toys, equipment and readily available materials. It will smell nice and not be overwhelmingly "cute." You might see real emotions, because even children have bad days sometimes; there might be tears or angry voices but there will also be a grown-up nearby, comforting, consoling, holding...

These are people who enjoy what they do and you can see it in their faces. They have created environments where children are able to get lost in curiosity and spend their days surrounded by discovery and wonder. Your heart will feel happy, your breathing will be calm, and your mind will be at ease. You will have found a good place.

When children are in environments that provide enough time each day for creating, moving, singing, discussing, observing, reading and playing they are able to engage in experiences that are strengthening the foundation that will prepare them for school. These are the preschools that are strengthening the foundation that supports the house of higher learning. The play-based programs are the ones that are "getting them ready" - not the ones with homework, computers and worksheets. Preschool is not the time nature set aside as boot camp for kindergarten. Right now children need to be creating, moving, singing, discussing, observing, reading and playing.

Trust your instincts, follow your heart, and resist the urge to start building a house where there is no foundation.

The house will fall down.

The Importance of Playing... In Review:

1. Child play is different than grown-up play.

2. Adults suffer from childhood amnesia.

3. Playing is learning and learning is playing.

4. The foundation of play supports the house of higher learning.

Some things to think about

1. Until this point had I really stopped to think about the amount of time children really need when playing?

2. Are we making enough time for playing?

3. Do we need to have more discussion in our school, center or home about the importance of play?

4. How did I play when I was little?

5. Who did I play with?

6. Am I suffering from childhood amnesia?

7. What is my understanding of play as "cement" in the context of the seven things serving as the foundation of the house of higher learning?

8. Am I able to articulate the importance of play in early childhood environments to those who ask?

9. Do we really believe in the power of play?

10. What is one thing I can do Monday to begin making more time each day to play?

Notable and Quotable

Play is the most useful tool for preparing children for the future and it's tasks.

-Bruno Bettelheim, *The Importance of Play*

Play helps youngsters get ready for the challenges of kindergarten.

-*The Orange County Register*, "The Focus is Preschool," April 9, 1997

Play is a frivolous wandering according to the whims of curiosity and interest, yet, to say that play has no inherent goal doesn't mean that its result cannot afterward be put to good purposes.

-*Sparks of Genius*

It may be more beneficial that a child should follow energetically some pursuit, of however trifling a nature, and thus acquire perseverance, than that he should be turned from it because of no further advantage to him.

-Charles Darwin

Part Three

Chapter 1

Challenges We Face...

My reason for writing this book was to expand on the reasons why the seven things need to be a part of your child's daily experience, whether your children are infants, toddlers, preschoolers, school-aged students, middle school students or college bound seniors. *It is never too late to increase the time we spend each day creating, moving, singing, discussing, observing, reading and playing.*

I think it would do the world a lot of good if we *all* spent more time doing these things! But my focus for this book was to show that when we make the time to do these things with young children, they go to school ready to learn, wanting more and excited about school.

The seven things of course is a guide, not a checklist. Please do not make a magnetic refrigerator chart with stickers and dry erase markers! Sing a song...check! Move around... check! Read a book... check! Instead start salt and peppering your day with a few of the suggested activities I have placed throughout the book. Remember the power of baby steps. It is hard to incorporate new things and as humans we are not too keen on change. Be patient and gentle with yourself and your family.

As we work together to increase the time we (and our schools) spend creating, moving, singing, discussing, observing, reading and playing it is important to know what our obstacles are and what stands in the way of making this happen. I thought it would be important to provide a brief outline of the major challenges we face when attempting to strengthen the play-based foundations that are supporting the houses of higher learning. My hope is that this list will assist us to work as a united front and allow us to have a collective understanding of the obstacles facing the creation of strong foundations and will allow each of us to apply our skills and talents to an area we can begin to change.

Challenges to...Creating

- Creating is often limited to the visual arts and other forms of creativity are not offered, noticed or encouraged.

- There is often no money for basic supplies such as paper, paint, crayons and markers.

- Lip service is paid to the importance of creativity via the implementation of arts based academic standards.

- Creativity Killers.

- Laminated Ladies.

Challenges to...Moving

- 40% of the schools in the United States have eliminated recess.

- Technology keeps children inside and in front of various screens (TV, movies, video games, computers) instead of outside where they are more active.

- Physical education requirements not being adhered to because of claims that the time is needed for more rigorous academic instruction.

- Removal of equipment from neighborhood playgrounds due to unnecessary (and often nonexistent) lawsuits.

- The myth that outside time is wasted time.

- Busy schedules interfere with informal outside playtime.

Challenges to...Singing

- Music is seen as an extracurricular "frill" thus it is usually the first program to be cut.

- We leave the singing up to the professionally recorded tapes and CDs and forget the power of our own voice.

- We have forgotten the words.

- We think we can't sing.

- We aren't aware of Gardner's work on the importance (and long lasting impact) of Musical Intelligence.

Challenges to...Discussing

- Not making time to have conversations with children.

- The flip from an emphasis on problem solving, communication and social skills to a more rigid academic agenda with an emphasis on testing and the regurgitation of facts.

- Computers and Television in cars, homes, bedrooms and classrooms.

- Talking AT children instead of talking WITH them.

- Impatience at the length of time it sometimes take children to express themselves.

Challenges to...Observing

- We look but do not see.

- We hear but do not listen.

- Liability issues and fears of lawsuits force schools to impose "no touching" rules despite the fact we know that humans need physical contact with each other.

- Sensory experiences are seen as messy activities with no real cognitive purpose or intellectual benefit.

- Hurried meals of pre-packaged convenience foods.

- Schools and childcare environments that reek of cleaning products instead of coffee, vanilla or cinnamon.

Challenges to...Reading

- School libraries are turning into computer labs.

- No money for new books.

- Librarians are being replaced with technology experts.

- Videos and computers are becoming the storytellers.

- Children aren't seeing grown-ups engaged in the reading of books.

- Not reading to children.

Challenges to...Playing

- No time.

- Don't understand the real value.

- It appears they aren't "doing anything."

- We have forgotten what it was like.

- A lack of awareness of the power that play has on the social, emotional, spiritual, cognitive and physical development of our children.

- Feeling the need to "defend" play instead of implementing it.

Chapter 2
Final Thoughts...

As long as we insist on building houses before there are foundations to support them and demand rigorous academic training before the children are ready, the houses of higher learning will crumble and collapse.

However, instead of stepping back and saying, "Hmmm, why do all these houses keep falling down?" we tend to push the children harder, starting everything younger and preparing for everything earlier while thinking, "Oh no, they weren't prepared! They weren't ready – they need something *more!*" - when that is the complete opposite of what they need! We mistakenly think they need something more, when really they just need something else.

Why do we continue to push? Are we worried that if they don't start learning now they will never want to? Do we worry they will want to "play" forever thus never obtain success? Go to college? Get a "good" job? I have met parents who have expressed concerns about how if the child does not attend X-Y-Z Preschool they will never get into Z-Y-X College. This is insane!

It is sad that parents have been somehow trained to think this way – even more disheartening, is that they believe it is true.

Remember that when the foundation is strong we can begin to build the house! Please know that children will seek this out! Remember my group of fours and fives from earlier in the book who said, "Teach us to read!" Wanting to read and write and to learn other academic subjects comes naturally when the process is allowed to unfold on it's own – *not when it is forced and pushed.*

We, as the grown-ups, in our hurried lifestyle and in our impatience, want from our children huge beautiful academic mansions. If we are not careful, we become very selfish and shortsighted and are unable to see that in our demand for a big house, we have neglected the foundation that will hold it up.

We must step back. Take a deep breath and take a good look at what is happening. Then we can begin to assess the situation in front of us and begin to change how things are being done. I am confident that this can happen.

Visit schools and watch what is happening in them. Many parents say that their preschool is excellent but it is the upper grades they are worried about. So go hang out there! Meet the teachers at the school your child will be attending. Get to know them. Talk with friends, family and parents about educational issues— many times people think "it's not my problem," but it is. Until the administrators and politicians know that you don't like what is happening, it will continue!

I am asked all the time, "Do you go to the capital and testify to the elected officials on behalf of the children and the schools?" Sure. But I'll be honest with you – I can rant and rave and share story after story after story – but the bottom line is that WE PUT THEM IN THOSE POSITIONS! Again, take the power back. If you don't like what's happening – do something about it! Write a letter to your elected officials and get five of your friends to write one with you, know the issues specifically related to education at election time and find out where the candidates stand, meet your child's principal, invite administration to your informal gatherings, put your child in a school that reflects your belief system, hang out in the classrooms more, homeschool, start a co-op...

Ghandi said, "Be the change you want to see in the world."

Start small, baby steps. Talk to a few parents, a few teachers. Let people know this is something you believe in – become vocal. Many are not involved in their child's education. I don't see how you can afford not to be. Many simply send their kids off to the neighborhood school and figure the rest is up to the teachers and staff. You must make a conscious choice to be involved. And by involved I mean *involved* – not just being willing to bake cookies for the holiday party. I mean – do you know if your child gets recess? When do they sing? What about art? How long is the lunch break? Are they outside at lunch, enjoying the break, eating and chatting with friends and then running around to blow off some steam? Or are they required to eat at their desks – a "working lunch," like little executives? What curriculum do they follow? What is the reading program? What is done when children need extra help? What is done when a child needs more challenges? Are they handled *individually* or forced to stay with the pack, thus not receiving what they need? At what grade does the testing frenzy begin? What engaging projects will now *stop* because they are "not on the test?" Do the teachers have a basic understanding of the learning styles, brain development and the ways in which children learn? Are they familiar with Howard Gardner's theory of Multiple Intelligences and then use this information to make the classroom engaging for *all* students? Or are we focused on the "3R's" and the rest of you be damned?

When you begin to get involved you find others who are involved and you start supporting one another. Your circle of support will grow bigger. We work together to change the schools and make sure that all the children are being given time each day to create, move, sing, discuss, observe, read and play.

Together we will overcome the challenges and will demand places of education when our child's success is no longer measured by grades, standardized test scores and exit exams. Instead, it will be measured by the thought behind their questions, the wonder on their faces, the magic in their eyes, the curiosity in their spirit, the persistence in their investigations, the laughter in their smiles and the compassion in their hearts.

We will have created children who are fun to be around and who can be serious when it is required of them. These children are compassionate and loving. They know how to solve problems (get their shovel back) appreciate books, songs and stories and are moved by beauty. Children who have been in environments that celebrate discovery and wonder become adults who do the same. But they are not yet adults. They are children. They are our responsibility. We become the guardians of inquiry. It is said that education is not the filling of a bucket, but rather the lighting of a fire. It is our job to keep that fire burning and to keep the flame alive.

Use that fire and passion to create that strong foundation. Frame it, pour it, allow it to set. Some will set faster than others. Some will take awhile. A long while. It can be hard to be patient while your neighbor is building a house and you are still waiting for your cement to dry. Your neighbor, mother in law, local politician, testing service agent and school board president all want to know why you don't have your house started yet. "Look at *our* houses!" they say.

So you look, and you get worried. You look at their big houses and then back at your wet mound of cement. Yet what they don't *say*, and what you don't see, is that in the dark of night, when no one was watching, they began building that house while the cement was still damp. Some never even laid the foundation down, but rather built a house in haste to impress the neighbors. "Why bother," they thought, "no one will know, and besides – I want my house up first!"

And while they might appear to be ahead of the game right now, guess what will happen in a year… or two… or five…

Their house will fall down.

"But, damn it!" you say! "My cement is just sitting there! It's not doing anything! And now – oh look! Now the frame is cracking! We are going to be here forever!"

Not forever – but for however long it takes.

Be patient. What does the cement need? A new frame? Provide it. Time? Provide it. More dry to offset the wet? Provide it. To be spread out again within the new frame? Provide it.

Granted you might wait, but in the long run who is benefiting the most? What is an extra six months? Eight months? Year? We're talking about the foundation that will be supporting them for the rest of their life! Why do we feel the need to hurry that up? We owe it to them to make it as strong as possible!

Don't rush it. Don't hurry.

Stop now and take a deep breath.

Inhale and exhale…

You will need to be focused, strong, articulate and brave. But we can do it. Together we can work to make it better. I share with you - you share with me. I support you – you support me. You support a friend – she supports her colleague. He supports the teachers and she supports the parent. I express my passion with you and you tell me of yours. I share with you the fire in my belly and you take some and use it to light your candle – then you share your light with someone who then shares with someone else.

A candle looses none of it's light by lighting another candle…together we can make the world a little brighter and do things a little bit better.

That's enough for today - let's get busy.

We can do this together.

All my best,

Lisa Murphy

NOTES

NOTES

Make time each day to...Create

1 These are a few of the many creative experiences provided in my first book, *The Ooey Gooey Handbook, Identifying and Creating Child Centered Environments*, for ordering information contact Learning Through Adventure at (800) 477-7977 or www.ooeygooey.com

2 Daniel Goleman, Paul Kaufman and Michael Ray, *The Creative Spirit*, (Dutton, New York), 1992 – the authors outline the "Creativity Killers" that were developed by Theresa Amabile.

3 From the handout for the workshop entitled, "Scribbles Suns to Humans: Watching it Happen" conducted by Sylvia Henry, California Association for the Education of Young Children Conference, March 2002. Her handout included the stages of scribbling as well as quotes from Rhoda Kellogg's work, *Analyzing Children's Art*. This reference is specifically from that cited work.

4 Notes from "Scribbles Suns and Humans" Workshop.

5 Daniel Goleman, Paul Kaufman and Michael Ray, *The Creative Spirit*, (Dutton, New York), 1992.

6 Ibid

7 Ilse Elisabeth Plattner, "Having Time for Children," *Child Care Information Exchange*, November 2001.

8 Daniel Goleman, Paul Kaufman and Michael Ray, *The Creative Spirit*, (Dutton, New York), 1992.

9 Personal notes from Alfie Kohn's keynote address at the California Association of Teachers of English (CATE) Conference, Ontario CA, February, 2001

10 Kathleen Kennedy Manzo, "Arts Programs Enhance Some Skills, Study Says," *Education Week*, 22 May 2002.

11 Robert Goldrich, "Art Reflects Life," *Shoot*, 9 February 2001.

12 Nanette Asimov, Jesse Hamlin, "Arts in classes rise from ashes. State providing money, settling student standards after decades of neglect", SF Gate, *San Francisco Chronicle,* 13 May 2002.

13 Professor Harold Hill is the "Music Man" character from the musical and movie of the same title. He waltzes into Gary, Indiana and attempts to establish a marching band filled with 76 trombones.. coronets.. ect while not having the "credentials" to do so. Great rental if you don't already know the flick. Check it out.

14 Nanette Asimov, Jesse Hamlin, "Arts in classes rise from ashes. State providing money, settling student standards after decades of neglect", SF Gate, *San Francisco Chronicle,* 13 May 2002.

15 BGS – Baby Gap Syndrome is in no way affiliated with the retail outlet! We just noticed that there was a pattern of these kids wearing lots of "Baby Gap" clothes. For the complete BGS article, check out Lisa's website, www.ooeygooey.com to reprint it or download it for your reference.

Make time each day to…Move

1 Robert and Michelle Root-Bernstein, *Sparks of Genius: Thirteen Thinking Tools of the World's Most Creative People,* (Houghton Mifflin, Boston), 1999.

2 Notes from Bev Bos' Good Stuff for Kids Conference, Roseville, California, Summers 1997, 1998, 2000, 2001.

3 Alison Armstrong, Charles Casement, *The Child and the Machine, How Computers Put Our Children's Education at Risk,* (Robins Lane Press, Batesville Maryland) 2000.

4 Notes taken from the "Smart Moves = Smart Learning" workshop presented by Sharron Krull and Eilene Green at the California Association for the Education of Young Children Conference, Long Beach, California, 1999.

5 Anna Mulrine, "What's your favorite class?", *U.S. News and World Report,* 1 May 2000; Walter Kirn, Wendy Cole, "What Ever Happened to Play?," *Time,* 30 April 2001; Kathleen Parker, "Kids Need Richness of Recess," *North County Times,* 11 April 1998 and www.allianceforchildhood.net

6 Katherine Schultz, "On the Elimination of Recess," *Education Week,* 10 June, 1998; "Educators Ponder Ending Recess" appeared in *The Michigan Daily,* 13 April 1998.

7   Personal phone conversation with Ms. Rebecca Lamphere, Play Advocate, Virginia Beach, VA, 2001 also Walter Kirn, Wendy Cole, "What Ever Happened to Play?," *Time*, 30 April 2001

8   Walter Kirn, Wendy Cole, "What Ever Happened to Play?," *Time*, 30 April 2001 also personal correspondence with Ms. Rebecca Lamphere

9   Kathleen Parker, "Kids Need Richness of Recess," *North County Times*, 11 April 1998

10 Joanne Oppenheim, "What's Happening to Recess?," *Good Housekeeping*, September, 1990.

11 Alison Armstrong, Charles Casement, *The Child and the Machine, How Computers Put Our Children's Education at Risk*, (Robins Lane Press, Batesville Maryland) 2000.

12 Sherry Posnick-Goodwin, "Isn't it Time to Treat Teachers as Professionals?," *California Educator*, March, 2002.

13 Joanne Oppenheim, "What's Happening to Recess?," *Good Housekeeping*, September, 1990.

14 American Academy of Pediatrics, "Clinical Practice Guideline: Treatment of the School-Aged Child With Attention-Deficit/Hyperactivity Disorder," October, 2001.

15 This figure was calculated using census 2000 information (available from www.census.gov) and American Academy of Pediatrics, "Clinical Practice Guideline: Treatment of the School-Aged Child With Attention-Deficit/Hyperactivity Disorder," October, 2001.

16 Sherry Posnick-Goodwin, "Fitness Boosts Brainpower," *California Educator*, November, 2002.

17 Carla Hannaford, Smart Moves – *Why Learning Is Not All In Your Head*, (Great Ocean Publishers, Arlington, Virginia), 1995.

18 Thomas Armstrong, *The Myth of the ADD Child*, (Plume Penguin, New York), 1995.

19 Naomi Aoki, "Narcolepsy drug eyed as alternative to Ritalin," *Boston Globe*, May 21, 2003.

20 Thomas Armstrong, *The Myth of the ADD Child*, (Plume Penguin, New York), 1995.

21 Ibid

22 Carla Hannaford, *Smart Moves – Why Learning Is Not All In Your Head*, (Great Ocean Publishers, Arlington, Virginia), 1995.

23 Thomas Armstrong, *The Myth of the ADD Child*, (Plume Penguin, New York), 1995.

24 Victoria Jean Dimidjian, *Play's Place in Public Education*, (National Education Association, Washington, D.C.) 1992

Make time each day to...Sing

1 Notes from Bev Bos' Good Stuff for Kids Conference, Roseville, California, Summers 1997, 1998, 2000, 2001

2 Ibid

3 Kathleen Cushman, "When Did the Singing Stop?" *Woman's Day*, June 23, 1992.

4 Mary Jeanette Howle, "Twinkle, Twinkle, Little Star: It's More Than Just a Nursery Song," *Children Today*, July/August, 1989.

5 Marvin Greenberg, *Your Children Need Music*, (Prentice Hall), 1979

6 Notes from Bev Bos' Good Stuff for Kids Conference, Roseville, California, Summers 1997, 1998, 2000, 2001

7 Notes from Bev Bos' "Memories and Traditions" workshop presented in Long Beach at the California Association for the Education of Young Children Conference, March 2002.

8 Carol Estes, "Lift Every Voice," *Utne Reader*, January/February 2002.

9 Mary Jeanette Howle, "Twinkle, Twinkle, Little Star: It's More Than Just a Nursery Song," *Children Today*, July/August, 1989.

10 Marvin Greenberg, *Your Children Need Music*, (Prentice Hall), 1979

11 Ibid

12 Notes from Bev Bos' "Memories and Traditions" workshop presented in Long Beach at the California Association for the Education of Young Children Conference, March 2002.

13 Mary Jeanette Howle, "Twinkle, Twinkle, Little Star: It's More Than Just a Nursery Song," *Children Today*, July/August, 1989.

Make time each day to...Discuss

1 Alison Armstrong, Charles Casement, *The Child and the Machine, How Computers Put Our Children's Education at Risk*, (Robins Lane Press, Batesville Maryland) 2000

2 Carla Hannaford, Smart Moves – *Why Learning Is Not All In Your Head*, (Great Ocean Publishers, Arlington, Virginia), 1995.

3 Ibid

4 Ibid

5 Alison Armstrong, Charles Casement, *The Child and the Machine, How Computers Put Our Children's Education at Risk*, (Robins Lane Press, Batesville Maryland) 2000

6 Carla Hannaford, Smart Moves – *Why Learning Is Not All In Your Head*, (Great Ocean Publishers, Arlington, Virginia), 1995.

7 Bruno Bettelheim, "The Importance of Play," *The Atlantic Monthly*, March,1987.

8 The Ewing Marion Kauffman Foundation, "Set For Success, Building a Strong Foundation for School Readiness Based on the Social-Emotional Development of Young Children," Summer 2002. Also visit www.emfk.org

9 Ibid

10 Clifford Stoll, *High Tech Heretic*, (Doubleday, New York) 1999.; and also referenced in John MacIntyre's, "Know Power" column in Southwest Airlines' *Spirit Magazine*, June 2002.

11 Susan Black, "How Do Your Children Grow?," *Executive Educator*, December, 1995. The original article, "Doing the Right Thing for Children: Linking Research and Policy Reform in the District of Columbia Public Schools," written by Rebecca Marcon appeared in *Young Children*, November, 1994.

12 Ronald Kotulak, "A Good Beginning: Sending America's Children to School With the Social and Emotional Competence They Need to Succeed", *Chicago Tribune*, 6 September 2000; The report, complied by the Child Mental Health Foundations and Agencies Network dated September 6, 2002 can be downloaded in full http://www.hhs.gov/whatsnew

13 Daniel Goleman, Paul Kaufman and Michael Ray, *The Creative Spirit*, (Dutton, New York), 1992.

14 Personal notes from Alfie Kohn's keynote address at the California Association of Teachers of English (CATE) Conference, Ontario CA, February, 2001.

15 Susan Black, "How Do Your Children Grow?," *Executive Educator*, 1995.

Make time each day to...Observe

1 Diane Ackerman, *A Natural History of the Senses*, (Random House, New York), 1990

2 Ibid

3 Ibid

4 Personal notes from Alfie Kohn's keynote address at the California Association of Teachers of English (CATE) Conference, Ontario CA, February, 2001.

Make time each day to...Read

1 Ellen Handler-Spitz, *Inside Picture Books*, (Yale University Press, New Haven, Conn.), 1999

2 Gladys Hunt, *Honey For a Child's Heart: The Imaginative Use of Books in Family Life*, (Zonderman Books, Grand Rapids, MI), 1989.

3 Mem Fox, Dear Mem Fox: *I Have Read All Your Books Even The Pathetic Ones*, (Penguin, Australia), 1990, 1992.

4 Mem Fox, *Reading Magic*, (Harcourt, San Diego), 2001.

5 Thomas Armstrong, *The Myth of the ADD Child*, (Plume Penguin, New York), 1995.

6 Dorothy Butler, Marie Clay, *Reading Begins At Home*, (Heineman Press), 1982.

7   Ibid

8   Gladys Hunt, *Honey For a Child's Heart: The Imaginative Use of Books in Family Life,* (Zonderman Books, Grand Rapids, MI), 1989.

9   Alison Armstrong, Charles Casement, *The Child and the Machine, How Computers Put Our Children's Education at Risk,* (Robins Lane Press, Batesville Maryland) 2000.

10 Susan Neuman, *What Research Reveals – Foundations for reading instruction in preschool and primary education,* U.S. Department of Education, October, 2002.

Make time each day to... Play

1   Notes from Bev Bos' Good Stuff for Kids Conference, Roseville, California, Summers 1997, 1998, 2000, 2001

2   Walter Kirn, Wendy Cole, "What Ever Happened to Play?," *Time*, 30 April 2001

3   This is the title of an article that appeared in *Childhood Education,* (volume 71, number 1, Fall 1994) and relates a kindergarten teacher's struggle in a classroom where play was not considered an appropriate medium for learning.

4   Walter Kirn, Wendy Cole, "What Ever Happened to Play?," *Time*, 30 April 2001

5   Robert and Michelle Root-Bernstein, *Sparks of Genius: Thirteen Thinking Tools of the World's Most Creative People,* (Houghton Mifflin, Boston), 1999.

6   Notes from Thomas Armstrong's lecture at the Parent Talk Series about "Multiple Intelligences", Thousand Oaks, CA, May 2002.

BIBLIOGRAPHY and SUGGESTED READINGS

Ackerman, Diane. *A Natural History of the Senses.* Random House: New York, 1990.

American Academy of Pediatrics, "Clinical Practice Guideline: Treatment of the School-Aged Child With Attention-Deficit/Hyperactivity Disorder," October, 2001.

Aoki, Naomi, "Narcolepsy Drug Eyed as Alternative to Ritalin," *Boston Globe*, May 21, 2003.

Armstrong, Alison & Casement, Charles. *The Child and the Machine.* Robins Lane Press: Maryland, 2000.

Armstrong, Thomas, *In Their Own Way.* Jeremy P. Tarcher/Putnam: New York, 2000.

Armstrong, Thomas. *7 Kinds of Smart.* Plume Penguin: New York, 1993, 1999.

Armstrong, Thomas. *The Myth of the A.D.D. Child.* Plume Penguin: New York, 1995.

Asimov, Nanette & Hamlin, Jesse. "Arts in classes rise from ashes. State spending money, settling student standards after decades of neglect, SF Gate, *San Francisco Chronicle*, 13 May 2002.

Ayers, William, *To Teach (first and second editions).* Teachers College Press: New York, 1994, 2001.

Barbour, Nita H. & Seefelst, Carol. *Developmental Continuity Across Preschool and Primary Grades.* Association for Childhood Education International: Maryland, 1993.

Beatty, Betty, *Preschool Education in America.* Yale University Press: New Haven and London,1995.

Bettelheim, Bruno. "The Importance of Play," *The Atlantic Monthly*, March, 1987.

Black, Susan. "How Do Your Children Grow?," *Executive Educator*, December, 1995.

Bly, Robert, *The Sibling Society.* Vintage Books: New York, 1977.

Brodsky Checnfeld, Mimi, *Teaching in the Key of Life.* NAEYC:

Washington, DC, 1993.

Butler, Dorothy & Clay, Marie. *Reading Begins At Home*, Heineman Press, 1982.

Campbell, Don. *The Mozart Effect*. Avon Books: New York, 1997.

Carroll, Lee, Tober, Jan, *The Indigo Children.* Hay House: Carlsbad, California, 1999.

Curtis, Deb, Carter, Margie, *The Art of Awareness.* Redleaf Press: Minnesota, 2000.

Cushman, Kathleen, "When Did the Singing Stop?" *Woman's Day*, June 23, 1992.

Dennison, Paul E., *Brain Gym, Teachers Edition.* Edu-Kinesthetics, Inc.: Ventura, California, 1989.

Dewey, John, *Experience and Education.* Collier Books: New York, 1938.

Diamond, Marion, *Magic Trees of the Mind.* Plume: New York, 1999.

Dimidjian, Victoria Jean. *Play's Place in Public Education*, National Education Association: Washington, D.C., 1992.

Elkind, David, *Miseducation – Preschoolers at Risk.* Alfred Knopf: New York, 1989.

Estes, Carol. "Lift Every Voice," *Utne Reader*, January/February, 2002.

Fox, Mem. *Dear Mem Fox I Have Read All Your Books Even The Pathetic Ones.* Penguin: Australia, 1990, 1992.

Fox, Mem. *Reading Magic.* Harcourt: San Diego, 2001.

Friel, John and Linda, *The 7 Worst Things Parents Do.* Health Communications, Inc: Deerfield Beach, Florida, 1999.

Fujawa, Judy, *Almost Everything You Need to Know About Early Childhood Education.* Gryphon House, Maryland, 1998.

Garbarino, James, *Raising Children in a Socially Toxic Environment.* Jossey-Bass: San Francisco, 1995.

Gardner, Howard, *The Unschooled Mind.* Basic Books: New York, 1991.

Gardner, Howard. *The Disciplined Mind.* Penguin: New York, 2000.

Garhart Mooney, Carol, *Theories of Childhood: Dewey, Montessori, Erikson, Piaget and Vygotsky*. Redleaf Press: Minnesota, 2000.

Goldman, H.H. *Review of General Psychiatry, second edition.* Appleton and Lange: San Mateo, Claifornia, 1988.

Goldrich, Robert. "Art Reflects Life," *Shoot*, 9 February 2001.

Goleman, Daniel, Kaufman, Paul & Ray, Michael. *The Creative Spirit.* Dutton: New York, 1992.

Gonzales-Mena, Janet, *Dragon Mom – Confessions of a Child-Development Expert.* Rattle OK Publications: Napa, California, 1995.

Gopnik, Alison, et al. *The Scientist in the Crib – What early learning tells us about the mind.* Perennial: New York, 2001.

Gosman, Fred G., *Spoiled Rotten – Today's children and how to change them.* Warner Books: New York, 1990.

Greenberg, Marvin. *Your Children Need Music*. Prentice Hall, 1979.

Gurewitz Clemens, Sydney, *The Sun's Not Broken, A Cloud's Just in the Way – On Child-Centered Teaching.* Gryphon House: Maryland, 1983.

Hainstock, Elizabeth, *The Essential Montessori*. Plume: New York, 1986.

Handler-Spitz, Ellen. *Inside Picture Books*. Yale University Press: New Haven, 1999.

Hannaford, Carla. *Smart Moves: Why Learning is Not All In Your Head.* Great Ocean Publishers: Arlington, VA, 1995.

Healy, Jane, *Failure to Connect – How computers affect our children's minds for better and worse.* Simon and Schuster: New York, 1998.

Healy, Jane. *Endangered Minds*. Simon & Schuster: New York, 1990.

Healy, Jane. *How To Have Intelligent and Creative Conversations With Your Kids*. Doubleday: New York, 1992.

Healy, Jane. *Your Child's Growing Mind*. Doubleday: New York, 1987, 1984.

Hern, Matt (ed.), *Deschooling Our Lives*. New Society: Philadelphia, 1996.

Howle, Mary Jeanette. "Twinkle, Twinkle, Little Star: It's More Than Just a Nursery Song," *Children Today*, July/August, 1989.

Hunt, Gladys. *Honey For a Child's Heart: The Imaginative Use of Books in Family Life.* Zonderman Books: Grand Rapids, MI, 1989.

Kennedy-Manzo, Kathleen. "Arts Programs Enhance Some Skills, Study Says," *Education Week*, 22 May 2002.

Kirn, Walter & Cole, Wendy. "What Ever Happened to Play?," *Time*, 30 April 2001.

Kohn, Alfie, *Punished By Rewards.* Houghton Mifflin: Boston, 1993.

Kohn, Alfie, *The Schools Our Children Deserve.* Houghton Mifflin: Boston, 1999.

Kohn, Alfie, *What To Look For In A Classroom… and other essays.* Jossey-Bass: San Francisco, 1998.

Kotulak, Ronald. "A Good Beginning: Sending America's Children to School With the Social and Emotional Competence They Need to Succeed", *Chicago Tribune*, 6 September 2000.

Mander, Jerry, *Four Arguments For the Elimination of Television.* Quill: New York, 1978.

Mate, Ferenc, *A Reasonable Life.* Albatross Publishing: New York, 1993.

McLaughlin, Emma, Kraus, Nicola. *The Nanny Diaries.* St. Martins Press: New York, 2002.

Montessori, Maria, *The Absorbent Mind.* Henry Holt: New York, 1995.

Mulrine, Anna. "What's your favorite class?", *U.S. News and World Report*, 1 May 2000.

Murphy, Lisa. *The Ooey Gooey Handbook – Identifying and Creating Child Centered Environments.* Learning Through Adventure: Carlsbad, CA, 2001.

Nabhan, Gary Paul, *The Geography of Childhood – Why children need wild places.* Beacon Press: Boston, 1994.

Neuman, Susan, *What Research Reveals – Foundations for reading instruction in preschool and primary education,* U.S. Department of Education, October, 2002.

Ohanian, Susan, *What Happened To Recess And Why Are Our Children Struggling In Kindergarten?* McGraw Hill: New York, 2002.

Oppenheim, Joanne. "What's Happening to Recess?," *Good Housekeeping,* September, 1990.

Paley, Vivian Gussin, *You Can't Say You Can't Play.* Harvard University Press: Cambridge, Mass., 1992.

Parker, Kathleen. "Kids Need Richness of Recess," *North County Times,* 11 April 1998

Pearce, Joseph Chilton. *Evolution's End. Claiming the Potential of Our Intelligence.* Harper: San Francisco, 1992.

Pipher, Mary, *Another Country – Navigating the emotional terrain of our elders.* Riverhead Books: New York, 1999.

Pipher, Mary, *Reviving Ophelia, Saving the Selves of Adolescent Girls.* Ballatine: New York, 1994.

Pipher, Mary. *The Shelter of Each Other.* Grosset/Putnam: New York, 1996.

Plattner, Ilse Elisabeth. "Having Time for Children," *Child Care Information Exchange,* November 2001.

Posnick-Goodwin, Sherry, "Fitness Boosts Brainpower," *California Educator,* November, 2002.

Posnick-Goodwin, Sherry. "Isn't it Time to Treat Teachers as Professionals?," *California Educator,* March, 2002.

Postman, Neil. *The End of Education.* Vintage Books: New York,1996.

Rivkin, Mary. *The Great Outdoors – Restoring Children's Right to Play Outside.* National Association for the Education of Young Children: Washington, DC, 1995.

Root-Bernstein, Robert & Michele. *Sparks of Genius: Thirteen Thinking Tools of the World's Most Creative People.* Houghton Mifflin: Boston, 1999.

Schultz, Katherine. "On the Elimination of Recess," *Education Week,* 10 June, 1998.

Segal, Marilyn, *Your Child At Play – Birth to one year.* Newmarket Press: New York, 1985.

Shandler, Sara, *Ophelia Speaks.* Harper Perennial: New York, 1999.

Shonkoff, Jack, Phillips, Deborah (eds.), *From Neurons to Neighborhoods.*

National Academy Press: Washington, DC, 2000.

Stoll, Clifford. *High Tech Heretic*. Doubleday: New York, 1999.

Taylor Gatto, John, *Dumbing Us Down*. New Society: Philadelphia, 1992.

The Ewing Marion Kauffman Foundation, *Set For Success, Building a Strong Foundation for School Readiness Based on the Social-Emotional Development of Young Children,* Summer 2002.

Walsh, David, *Selling Out America's Children*. Fairview Press: Minneapolis, 1994.

Weisman Topal, Cathy, Gandini, Lella, *Beautiful Stuff! Learning With Found Materials!* Davis Publications: Worcester, Mass, 1999.

NOTES

NOTES

NOTES

NOTES

NOTES

NOTES

NOTES

NOTES

NOTES

NOTES

NOTES